CAMBRIDGE
UNIVERSITY PRESS

Cambridge Lower Secondary
Science

WORKBOOK 7

Mary Jones, Diane Fellowes-Freeman & Michael Smyth

CAMBRIDGE
UNIVERSITY PRESS

University Printing House, Cambridge CB2 8BS, United Kingdom

One Liberty Plaza, 20th Floor, New York, NY 10006, USA

477 Williamstown Road, Port Melbourne, VIC 3207, Australia

314–321, 3rd Floor, Plot 3, Splendor Forum, Jasola District Centre, New Delhi – 110025, India

79 Anson Road, #06–04/06, Singapore 079906

Cambridge University Press is part of the University of Cambridge.

It furthers the University's mission by disseminating knowledge in the pursuit of education, learning and research at the highest international levels of excellence.

www.cambridge.org
Information on this title: www.cambridge.org/9781108742818

© Cambridge University Press 2021

This publication is in copyright. Subject to statutory exception

and to the provisions of relevant collective licensing agreements,

no reproduction of any part may take place without the written

permission of Cambridge University Press.

First published 2012

Second edition 2021

20 19 18 17 16 15 14 13 12 11 10 9 8 7 6 5 4 3 2 1

Printed in Malaysia by Vivar Printing

A catalogue record for this publication is available from the British Library

ISBN 978-1-108-74281-8 Paperback with Digital Access (1 year)

Cambridge University Press has no responsibility for the persistence or accuracy of URLs for external or third-party internet websites referred to in this publication, and does not guarantee that any content on such websites is, or will remain, accurate or appropriate. Information regarding prices, travel timetables, and other factual information given in this work is correct at the time of first printing but Cambridge University Press does not guarantee the accuracy of such information thereafter.

Cambridge International copyright material in this publication is reproduced under licence and remains the intellectual property of Cambridge Assessment International Education.

The exercises in this Workbook have been written to cover the Biology, Chemistry, Physics, Earth and Space and any appropriate Thinking and Working Scientifically learning objectives from the Cambridge Lower Secondary Science curriculum framework (0893). Some Thinking and Working Scientifically learning objectives and the Science in Context learning objectives have not been covered in this Workbook.

NOTICE TO TEACHERS IN THE UK
It is illegal to reproduce any part of this work in material form (including photocopying and electronic storage) except under the following circumstances:
(i) where you are abiding by a licence granted to your school or institution by the Copyright Licensing Agency;
(ii) where no such licence exists, or where you wish to exceed the terms of a licence, and you have gained the written permission of Cambridge University Press;
(iii) where you are allowed to reproduce without permission under the provisions of Chapter 3 of the Copyright, Designs and Patents Act 1988, which covers, for example, the reproduction of short passages within certain types of educational anthology and reproduction for the purposes of setting examination questions.

> Contents

1 Cells
1.1	Plant cells	1
1.2	Animal cells	5
1.3	Specialised cells	7
1.4	Cells, tissues and organs	11

2 Materials and their structure
2.1	Solids, liquids and gases	16
2.2	Changes of state	21
2.3	Explaining changes of state	26
2.4	The water cycle	30
2.5	Atoms, elements and the Periodic Table	32
2.6	Compounds and formulae	34
2.7	Compounds and mixtures	38

3 Forces and energy
3.1	Gravity, weight and mass	42
3.2	Formation of the Solar System	48
3.3	Movement in space	52
3.4	Tides	55
3.5	Energy	59
3.6	Changes in energy	63
3.7	Where does energy go?	66

4 Grouping and identifying organisms
4.1	Characteristics of living organisms	70
4.2	Viruses	74
4.3	What is a species?	76
4.4	Using keys	81
4.5	Writing keys	87

5 Properties of materials

5.1	Metals and non-metals	89
5.2	Comparing metals and non-metals	92
5.3	Metal mixtures	97
5.4	Using the properties of materials to separate mixtures	99
5.5	Acids and alkalis	103
5.6	Indicators and the pH scale	105

6 Earth physics

6.1	Sound waves	109
6.2	Reflections of sound	112
6.3	The structure of the Earth	118
6.4	Changes in the Earth	120
6.5	Solar and lunar eclipses	122

7 Microorganisms in the environment

7.1	Microorganisms	125
7.2	Food chains and webs	129
7.3	Microorganisms and decay	133
7.4	Microorganisms in food webs	140

8 Changes to materials

8.1	Simple chemical reactions	142
8.2	Neutralisation	147
8.3	Investigating acids and alkalis	152
8.4	Detecting chemical reactions	161

9 Electricity

9.1	Flow of electricity	164
9.2	Electrical circuits	166
9.3	Measuring the flow of current	168
9.4	Conductors and insulators	170
9.5	Adding and removing components	172

> How to use this book

This workbook provides questions for you to practise what you have learned in class. There is a topic to match each topic in your Learner's Book. Each topic contains the following sections:

Focus: these questions help you to master the basics

Focus
This exercise will help you to check that you understand what the term 'species' means.
Complete the sentences on the next page.
Choose from these words or phrases.
You can use each word or phrase once, more than once or not at all.

different to   exactly the same as   fight   fertile   healthy
horn   horns   infertile   kingdoms   reproduce   species

The drawings show a white rhinoceros and an Indian rhinoceros.

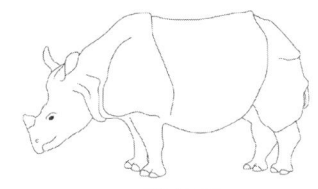

Indian rhinoceros

white rhinoceros

Practice: these questions help you to become more confident in using what you have learned

Practice
2 Scientists do not all agree about whether viruses are living organisms.

Viruses are living organisms.

I do not agree that viruses should be classed as living organisms.

A   B

a Write down **one** piece of information about viruses that supports the view of Scientist **A**.

....

Challenge: these questions will make you think very hard

Challenge
In this task, you will use your understanding of what makes a separate species. You will suggest how scientists could decide how to classify a newly discovered kind of frog.

In 2016, a team of researchers from India and the National University of Singapore discovered an unusual frog in a rocky habitat near the coast of southwest India.

The frog is tiny – only about 16mm long. It looks similar to other little frogs that are classified in the genus *Microhyla*. This frog is pale brown and has black and orangey-red markings on its back, feet and sides. The males make a call that sounds like a cricket chirping.

› Acknowledgements

The authors and publishers acknowledge the following sources of copyright material and are grateful for the permissions granted. While every effort has been made, it has not always been possible to identify the sources of all the material used, or to trace all copyright holders. If any omissions are brought to our notice, we will be happy to include the appropriate acknowledgements on reprinting.

Thanks to the following for permission to reproduce images:

Cover Mehmet Hilmi Barcin/GI; *Inside* Unit 3 SCIEPRO/GI; Daniel Dickman/GI; Print Collector/GI; Universal History Archive/GI; Unit 4 Buena Vista Images/GI; Suneet Bhardwaj/GI; by kind permission of Seshadri K.S; Jill Ferry/GI; Corbis/VCG/GI; Geoff Jones (x2), Unit 7 Staffan Widstrand/GI; Maxime Riendeau/GI; John Joslin/500px/GI; Unit 8 Raymond Gehman/GI; NoSystem images/GI

GI = Getty Images

1 Cells

> 1.1 Plant cells

Exercise 1.1A Structure of a plant cell

Focus

This exercise will help you to learn the names of the parts of a plant cell.

Complete the labels on the plant cell.

Use these words.

cell wall   cell membrane   cytoplasm   mitochondrion
nucleus   sap vacuole   chloroplast

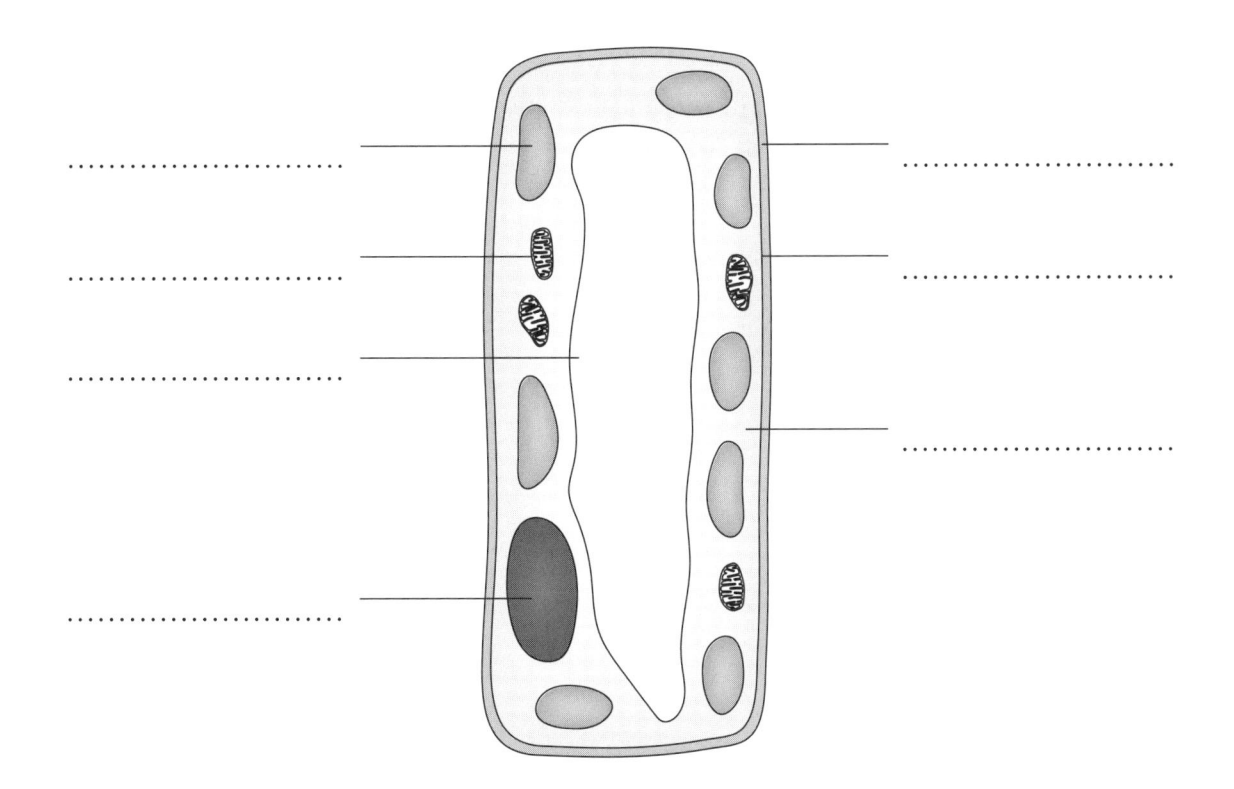

1 Cells

Exercise 1.1B Drawing and labelling a plant cell

Practice

In this exercise, you will practise making and labelling a clear, simple diagram.

Marcus makes a drawing of a plant cell.

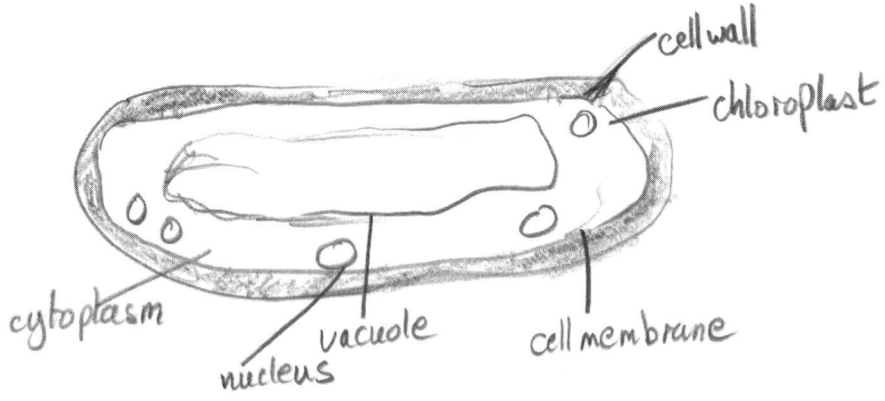

Labels on drawing: cell wall, chloroplast, cytoplasm, nucleus, vacuole, cell membrane

Marcus's teacher gives him a list of three things he needs to do, to improve his drawing.

- Make sure each label line touches the structure it is labelling

- Take care to get the shapes and proportions correct

- Do not shade or colour your drawing.

1.1 Plant cells

1   Write down **two** more ways that Marcus can improve his labels.

    ....

    ....

2   In the space below, draw and label a better diagram of the same plant cell.

1 Cells

Exercise 1.1C Different plant cells

Challenge

In this exercise, you will practise making comparisons.
You will also think about why plant cells are not all the same.

The diagrams show two plant cells.

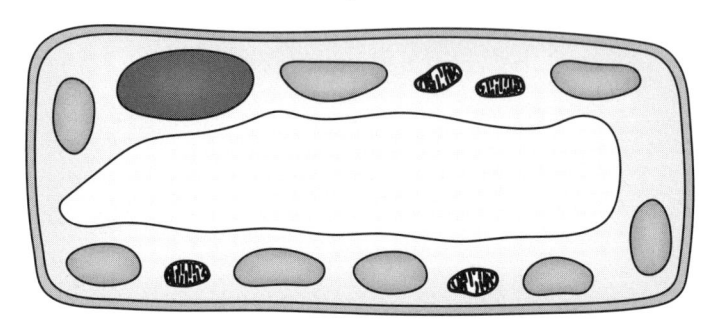

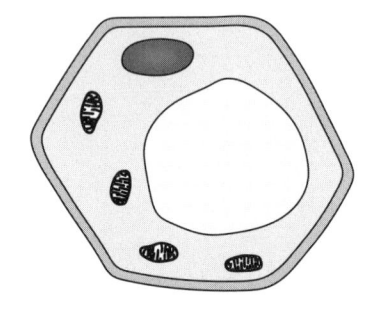

Plant cell **A**.   Plant cell **B**.

1   Describe **three** differences between Plant cell **A** and Plant cell **B**.

    The first difference has been started for you.

    First difference: Plant cell A has ....

    but Plant cell B ....

    ....

    Second difference:

    ....

    ....

    Third difference:

    ....

    ....

2   Suggest which cell comes from a leaf.

    Explain your suggestion.

    ....

    ....

> 1.2 Animal cells

Exercise 1.2 How to use a microscope

Some of the things that biologists study are very small. Answering these questions will help you to become confident in using a microscope to see very small things.

Focus

1   The diagram shows a microscope.

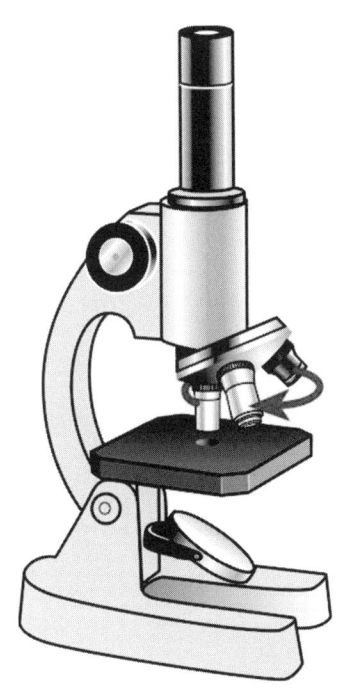

Label the parts of the microscope. Use all of the words in this list.

stage   eyepiece   mirror   high-power objective lens
medium-power objective lens   low-power objective lens
coarse focusing knob   fine focusing knob

1 Cells

Practice

2 Zara is using a microscope to look at some animal cells on a slide. She knows that there are animal cells on the slide but when she looks through the microscope, she cannot see any cells.

List **three** possible reasons why Zara cannot see any cells.

First reason: ....

Second reason: ....

Third reason: ....

Challenge

3 Write some advice to Zara, to help her to see the cells on her slide.

....

....

....

....

....

....

....

....

> 1.3 Specialised cells

Exercise 1.3 How cells are specialised for their functions

This exercise will help you to explain how cells are specialised for their functions. For Question 3a you will need to think hard about designing a table that is easy for everyone to understand. It is a good idea to try out several ideas on rough paper first.

Focus

1 The diagram shows a red blood cell.

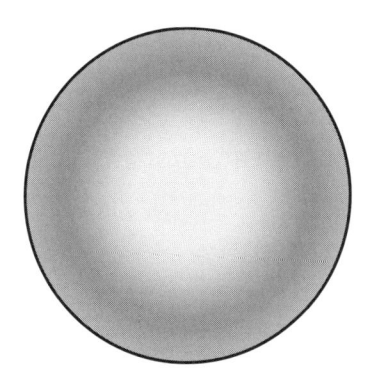

Complete the sentences.

Choose words from the list.

You can use each word once, more than once or not at all.

capillaries   cytoplasm   food   haemoglobin   oxygen

a Red blood cells contain a substance called

.... This helps them to carry

.... around the body.

b Red blood cells are smaller than most cells. This helps them to squeeze through the small blood vessels called

....

1 Cells

Practice

2 The diagram shows a specialised cell.

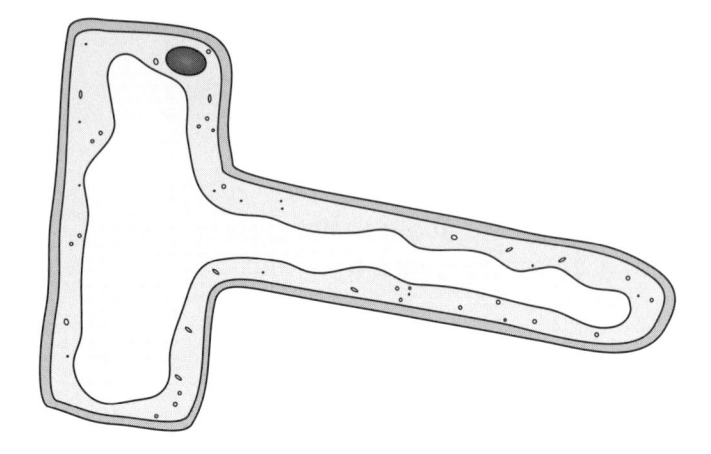

a Name this cell.

　　　………………………………………………………………………………

b Explain how you can tell that this is a plant cell and not an animal cell.

　　　………………………………………………………………………………

　　　………………………………………………………………………………

c Describe the function of this cell.

　　　………………………………………………………………………………

　　　………………………………………………………………………………

d Explain how this cell is adapted for its function.

　　　………………………………………………………………………………

　　　………………………………………………………………………………

　　　………………………………………………………………………………

Challenge

3 The diagrams show two specialised cells.

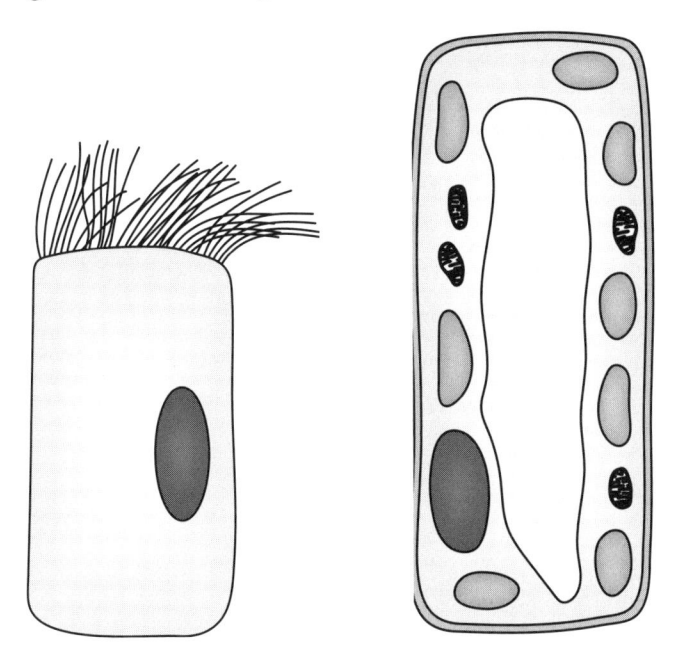

a Design and draw a table that you can use to compare the structures of these two cells.

Then complete your table.

1 Cells

b In your own words, explain how the structure of each cell is adapted for its function.

....

....

....

....

....

....

....

....

....

> 1.4 Cells, tissues and organs

Exercise 1.4A Identifying cells, tissues, organs and organ systems

Focus

This exercise will help you to remember the meanings of the words 'cell', 'tissue', 'organ' and 'organ system'.

Draw a line from each word to the correct diagram.

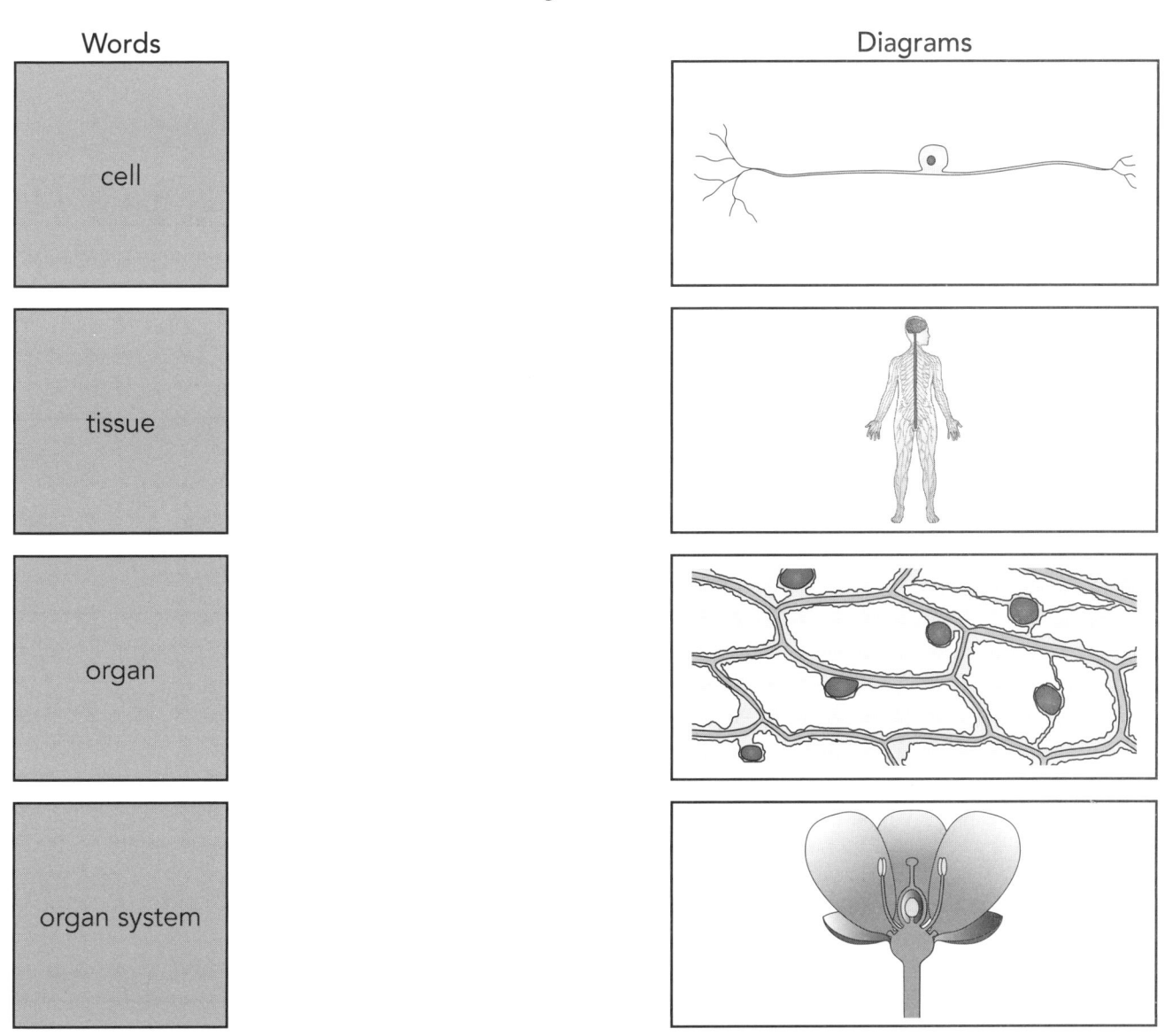

Words

- cell
- tissue
- organ
- organ system

Diagrams

1 Cells

Exercise 1.4B Human organ systems

Practice

If you studied Cambridge Science before Stage 7, you will have learnt about some of the organ systems in the human body. This will help you to complete the table. If you cannot fill in the third column from memory, look up the organ systems on the internet or in the library.

The table below is about four organ systems in the human body. These are:

respiratory system   **nervous system**
circulatory system   **digestive system**

Complete the table by:

- writing the name of the organ system in the second column
- writing at least **two** organs in the third column.

Function	Organ system	Some organs in the system
transporting substances around the body		
breaking down food and absorbing it into the blood		
taking oxygen into the body and getting rid of carbon dioxide		
helping different parts of the body to communicate with one another		

Exercise 1.4C Sting cells in *Hydra*

Challenge

In this challenging task, you will practise finding relevant information in text and diagrams. You will then apply this information, and your knowledge of cells, tissues and organs, to answer questions.

Hydra is a tiny animal that lives in freshwater ponds. It has tentacles that it uses to catch even smaller animals, which it pushes into its mouth. The mouth opens into a cavity where digestion takes place.

The body of *Hydra* is made up of two layers of cells. The diagram shows what *Hydra* would look like if you cut one in two, from top to bottom, and looked at it through a microscope.

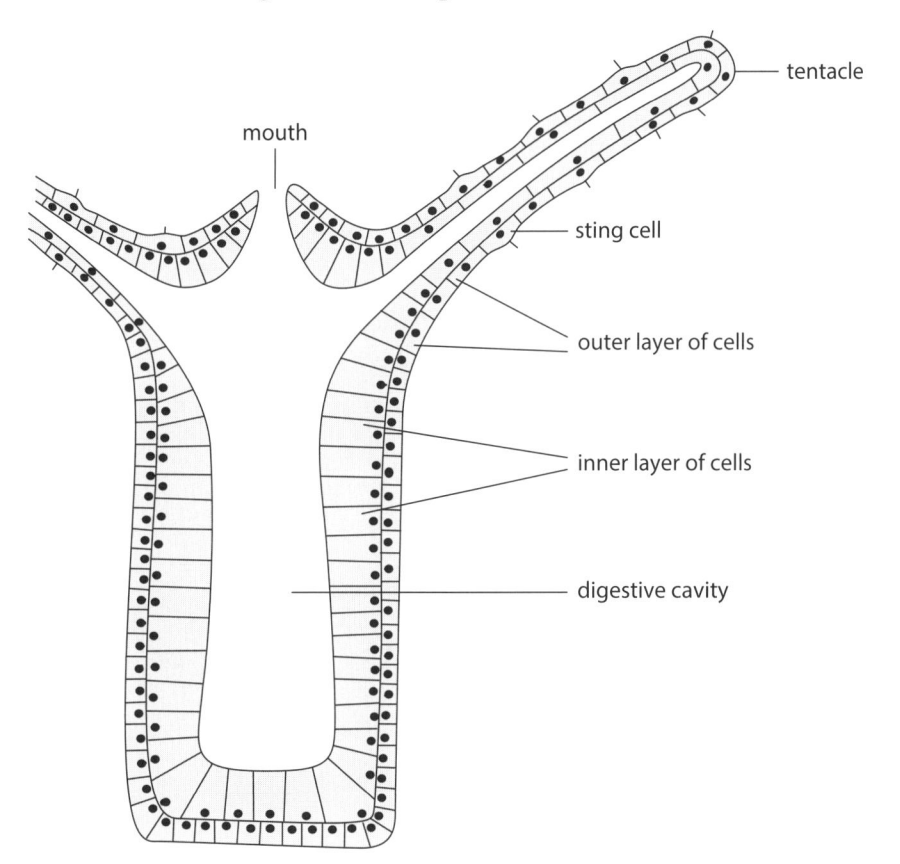

1 Cells

Hydra has some specialised cells, called sting cells, to help it to catch its food.

These cells contain tiny coiled threads. When a prey animal touches the trigger on the sting cell, the thread shoots out and wraps around the prey. Some of these threads may have poisonous chemicals on them, which kill the prey.

The diagram shows a sting cell before and after it has been triggered.

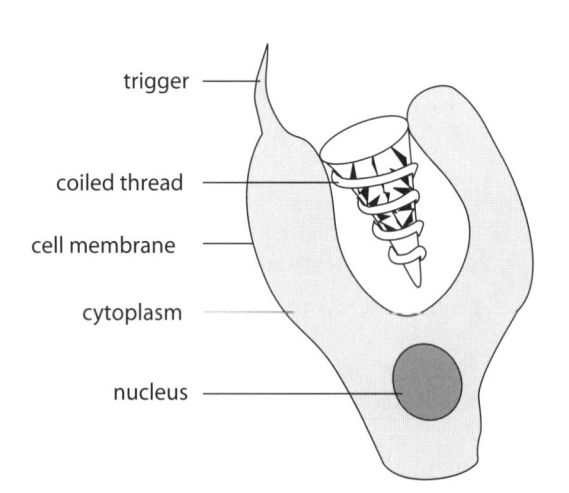

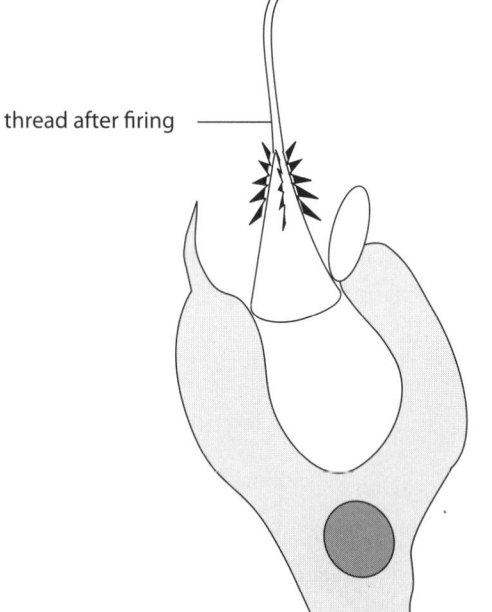

1 For each of these parts of *Hydra*, decide whether it is a cell, a tissue or an organ.

   a inner layer of cells ....

   b outer layer of cells ....

   c sting cell ....

   d tentacle ....

2 In humans, there are several different organs that make up the digestive system.

Does *Hydra* have a digestive system? Explain your answer.

....

....

....

1.4 Cells, tissues and organs

3 List **three** features of a sting cell that you would expect to find in most animal cells.

....

....

....

4 Explain how you can tell from the diagram that the sting cell is an animal cell and not a plant cell.

....

....

....

5 A sting cell is a specialised cell. In your own words, explain how a sting cell is adapted for its function.

....

....

....

....

....

....

....

2 Materials and their structure

> 2.1 Solids, liquids and gases

Exercise 2.1A Sorting solids, liquids and gases

Focus

This exercise will help you to check that you understand the properties of solids, liquids and gases.

Zara makes a cake with icing for her family.

powered sugar
beaten eggs
water
FLOUR
MILK
SUGAR
BUTTER
food colouring

2.1 Solids, liquids and gases

Here are the items she needs.

1   Write the name of each item Zara needs in the correct column of the table.

Solids	Liquids

2   Here are some more items. Add their names to your table above. You need to add a column to the table for gases.

   •   Draw with a pencil and use a ruler.
   •   Give the new column a heading.
   •   Make the column as wide as the others.

water
cooking pan
butane gas burner

flame
candle

17

2 Materials and their structure

Exercise 2.1B Solid, liquid or gas?

Practice

In this exercise you will practise using and interpreting information from a table.

Arun has been asked to test five materials to see if they are solid, liquid or gas. He has carried out some simple tests on some of the materials. He has not yet completed his tests.

This is his results table.

Material	Can it be compressed?	Does it flow?	Does it stay the same shape?	Does the volume stay the same?
A	yes	yes		
B		yes		yes
C		yes		
D		yes		yes
E				yes

1 Is material A a solid, a liquid or a gas? Explain your answer.

   ....

   ....

   ....

2 Is material B a solid, a liquid or a gas? Explain your answer.

   ....

   ....

   ....

2.1 Solids, liquids and gases

3 Arun thinks that material C is either a liquid or a gas.
Which **one** other test would you carry out to find out which it is?
Explain your choice.

....

....

....

4 Arun thinks material D is a liquid. Is he correct? Explain the reason for your answer.

....

....

....

5 Arun knows that material E is not a gas. Explain how he knows this.

....

....

6 What test should he do to decide if material E is a liquid or a solid?
Explain your answer.

....

....

2 Materials and their structure

Exercise 2.1C Properties of solids, liquids and gases

Challenge

In this exercise, you will consider observations of some unusual behaviour of a solid. Then you will discuss and explain the reasons for these observations.

Flour is a solid, but it is in powder form. When Marcus was baking, he observed that the flour had the properties shown here.

A He poured it.

B He found it took the shape of the container.

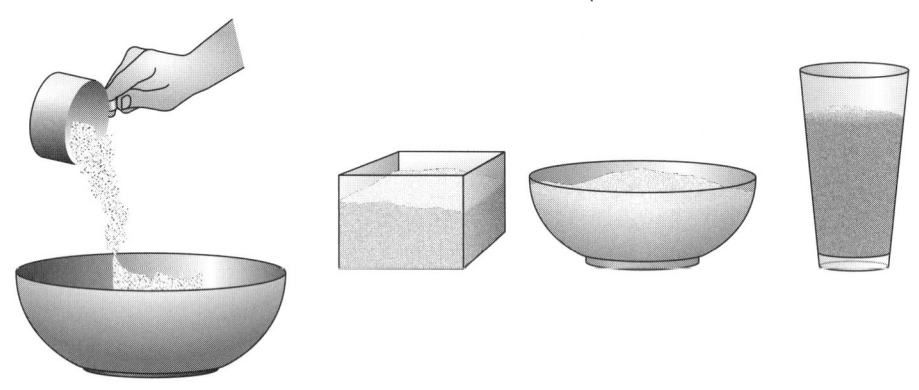

C When he tapped the container of flour on the table, the flour took up less space.

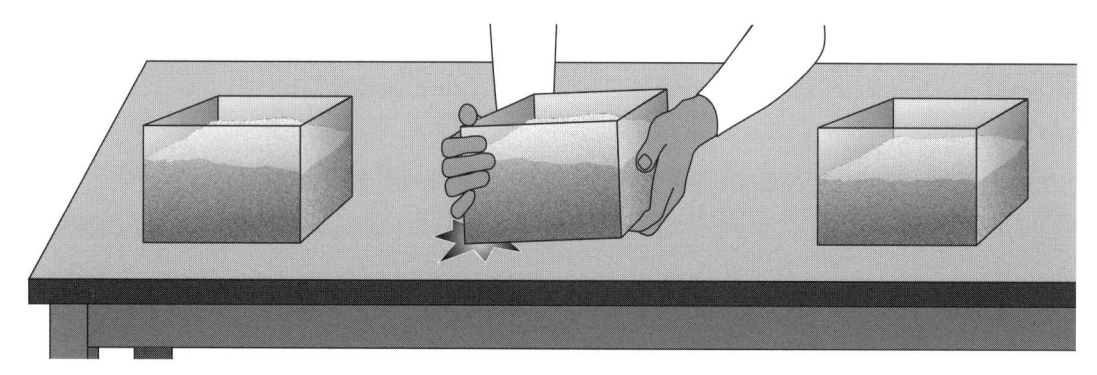

The properties shown in diagrams **A**, **B** and **C** are not usually those of a solid.

1   Write down which state(s) of matter you would expect to have the property shown in:

   A   ....

   B   ....

2   Explain why the flour has the property shown in:

    A   ....

        ....

        ....

    B   ....

        ....

        ....

    C   ....

        ....

        ....

> 2.2 Changing state

Exercise 2.2 Marcus's water heating investigation

In this exercise, you will practise drawing a table, then use it to record the results of an investigation and plot a graph.

Focus

Marcus carries out an experiment to investigate what happens to the temperature of water when it is heated.

He first measures the **temperature** of the water in the beaker (at 0 minutes).

Then he heats the water.

He measures the temperature every minute.

He does this for ten minutes.

2 Materials and their structure

1 What safety precautions is Marcus taking?

....

2 Draw a table below for Marcus to record his results.

3 The diagrams show Marcus's thermometer after different times. Write the temperatures in the spaces provided.

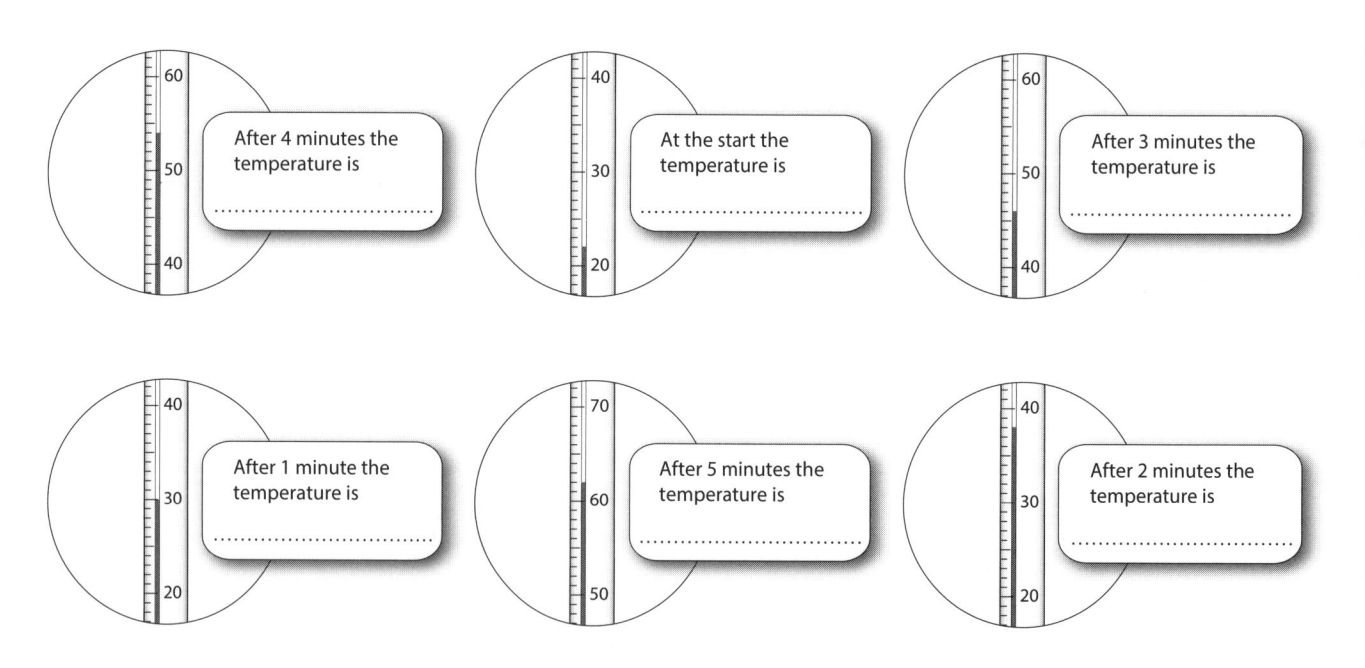

After 4 minutes the temperature is ....

At the start the temperature is ....

After 3 minutes the temperature is ....

After 1 minute the temperature is ....

After 5 minutes the temperature is ....

After 2 minutes the temperature is ....

4 Write the results into your table. Remember, the results need to be in order of the timings.

2.2 Changing state

5 Use your table of results from the previous question to plot a graph.

First label the axes with the **units**: time in minutes and temperature in °C.

Then plot each point carefully. The first one has been done for you.

Remember to use a pencil. Find the time on the horizontal axis. Go upwards until you come to the correct temperature. Mark with a small cross.

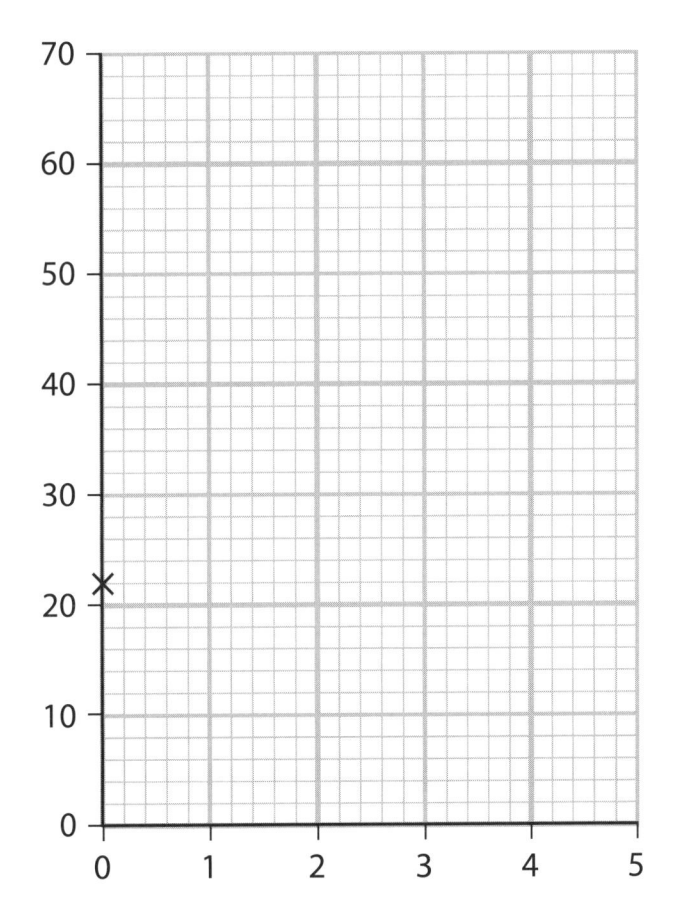

Look carefully at the points you have plotted. Use your ruler to see whether they form a straight line. Draw a straight line that passes through as many points as possible.

6 Write a sentence about what the graph shows.

....

....

2 Materials and their structure

Practice

7 Zara, a student in Marcus's class, has plotted her results on a graph.

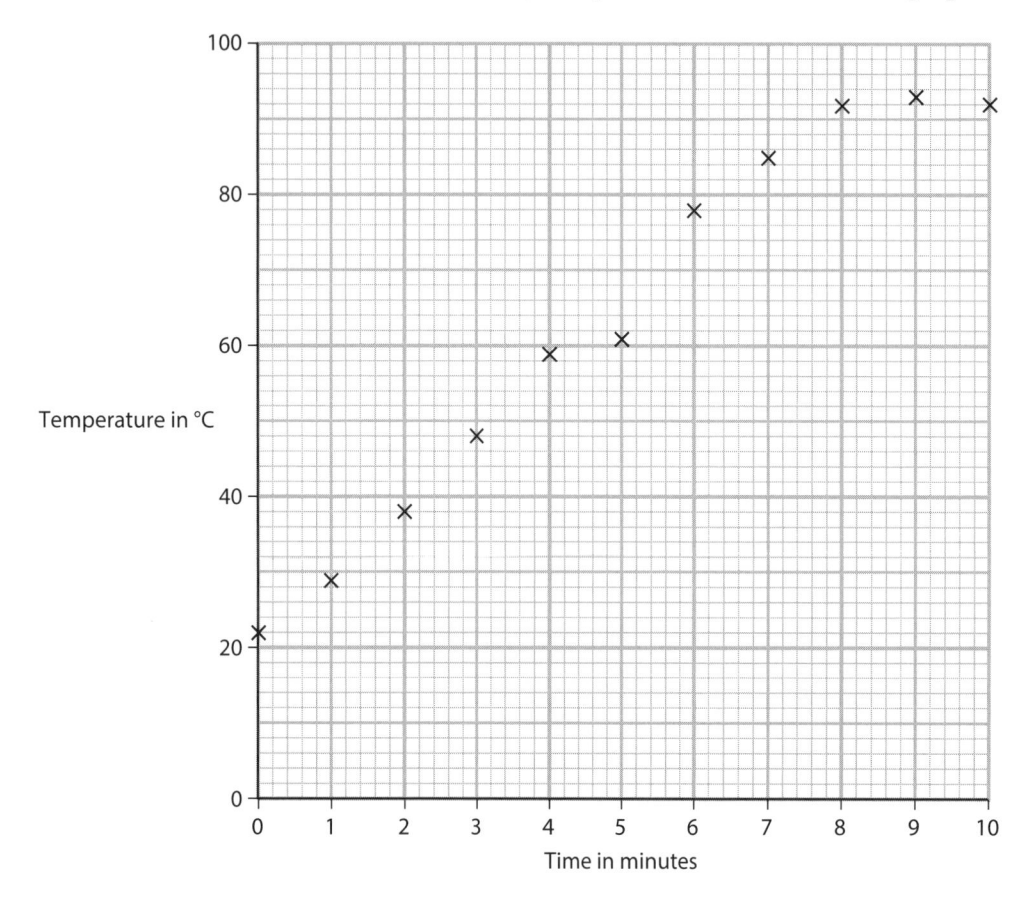

Temperature in °C (y-axis, 0 to 100)
Time in minutes (x-axis, 0 to 10)

Plotted points approximately: (0, 22), (1, 28), (2, 38), (3, 48), (4, 58), (5, 61), (6, 78), (7, 85), (8, 92), (9, 93), (10, 92).

a One of the points on the graph does not fit the pattern. Draw a circle around it.

b Suggest what Zara should do about this result.

....

....

8 Look at the graph Zara drew.

Carefully look at the pattern the points make on the graph.

Can you see that they follow a curve?

Using a sharp pencil, draw a smooth line that follows this curve. The line does not need to go through every point. There should be approximately the same number of points above your curve as below it.

This is called a **line of best fit**.

2.2 Changing state

9   Write a sentence to describe what the graph shows.

    ....

    ....

Challenge

10 Explain what happens to the temperature of the liquid as it is heated.

    ....

    ....

    ....

11 Zara measured the volume of the liquid at the start and the end of the investigation.

    a   Do you think the volume of liquid at the end was the same as at the beginning?

        ....

    b   What is the reason for your answer?

        ....

        ....

        ....

        ....

2 Materials and their structure

> 2.3 Explaining changes of state

Exercise 2.3A Change of state

Focus

In this exercise, you will explain what happens when a liquid and a solid change state.

Diagram **A** shows the particles in a liquid.

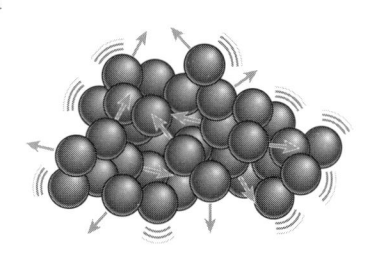

1   Complete this sentence.

   If the particles in diagram **A** lose enough energy, the liquid

   will change state and become a ....

A Particles in a liquid

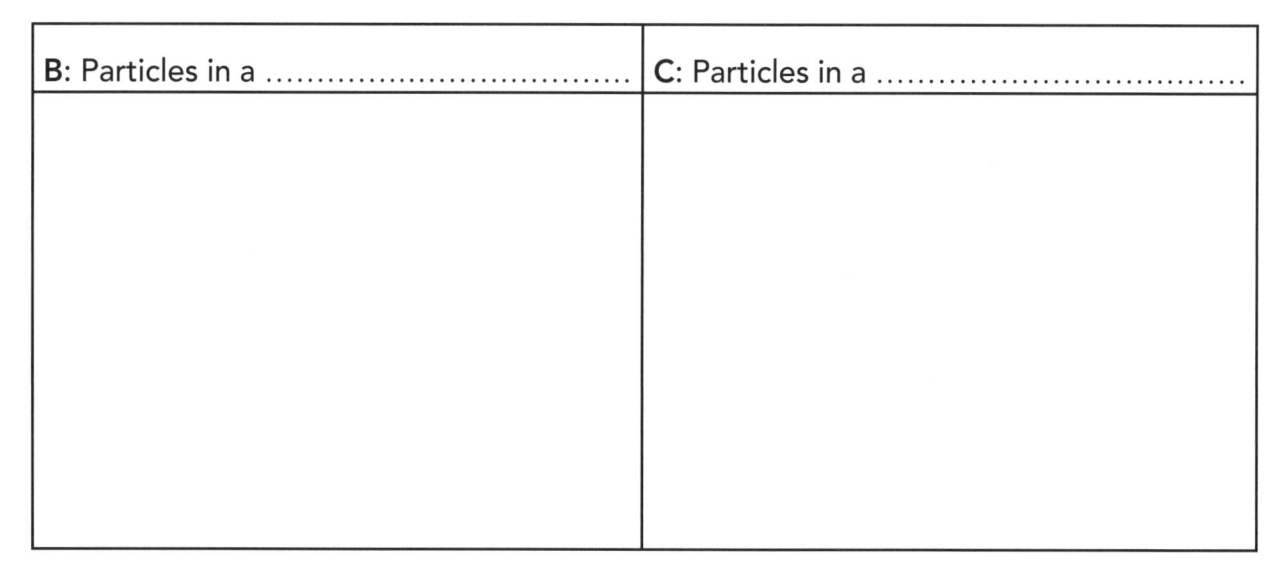

2   In box **B** below, draw the particles after this change of state. Complete the heading.

B: Particles in a	**C:** Particles in a ....

3   Complete this sentence.

   If the particles in diagram **A** gain enough energy, the liquid will

   change state and become a ....

4   In box **C**, draw the particles after this change of state. Complete the heading.

2.3 Explaining changes of state

5 Draw a circle around the correct word or words in these sentences.

For a solid to melt, the particles must **gain / lose** energy.

The particles vibrate **less / more**.

The particles have enough energy to escape the **strong / weak** forces holding them in their places.

The particles can now move **away from / past** each other.

The solid has changed state and become a **liquid / gas**.

6 Write one of these words in each of the spaces on the diagram to name the change that is taking place.

melting   freezing   condensing   boiling

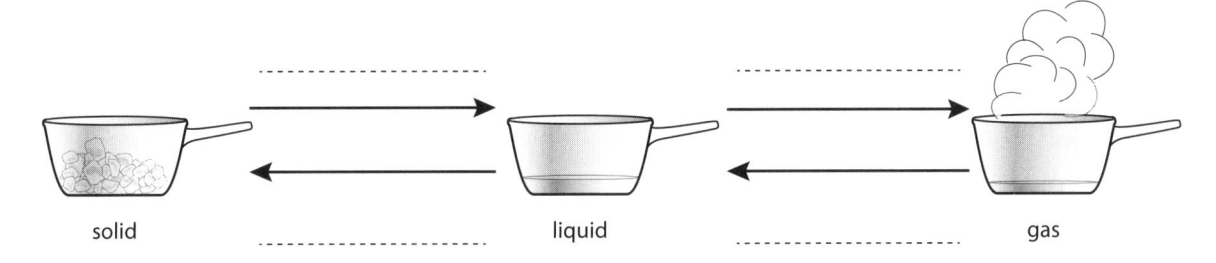

Exercise 2.3B Particle theory and change of state

Practice

This exercise will help you to understand and remember particle theory. Remember that 'explaining' something means that you have to say not only **what** happens, but also **how** or **why** it happens!

1 Explain, in terms of particle theory, what happens when ice is heated and melts to form water.

....

....

2 Materials and their structure

2 When the solid iron bar in the diagram is heated, it no longer fits the holder.

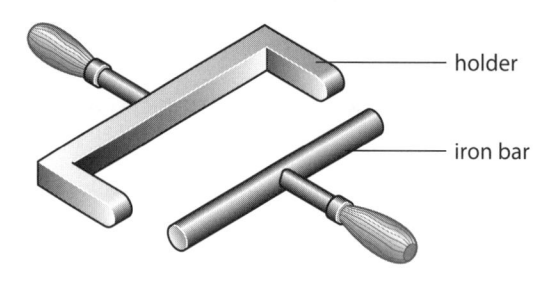

Use particle theory to explain why this happens.

....

....

3 Use the terms below to match each of the statements **a** to **g**.
Each word may be used once, more than once or not at all.

boil   compressed   condensation   evaporation   gas   heat
liquid   freeze   solid   vibrate   melting   move

a A state of matter where the particles do not touch each other:

....

b When a gas is cooled to form a liquid: ....

c Particles in solids, liquids and gases do this:

....

d Solid changing to a liquid: ....

e When a liquid changes into a gas: ....

f The particles in liquids and gases can do this:

....

g The state of matter that can be compressed:

....

Exercise 2.3C Explaining changes of state

Challenge

This exercise gives you practice in using particle theory to explain changes of state.

Use the correct scientific vocabulary in your explanations.

1   Use particle theory to explain what happens when a solid is heated and it changes into a liquid.

    ....

    ....

    ....

    ....

2   Use particle theory to explain what happens when a gas reaches a cold surface and it changes into a liquid.

    ....

    ....

    ....

    ....

3   Use particle theory to explain what happens when a liquid is heated and it changes into a gas.

    ....

    ....

    ....

    ....

2 Materials and their structure

4   Look back at your answers and think about the scientific words you have used. Are there any more that you should have included?

    ....

    ....

> 2.4 The water cycle

Exercise 2.4 The water cycle

In this exercise, you will label a diagram of the water cycle and explain some of the processes involved.

Focus

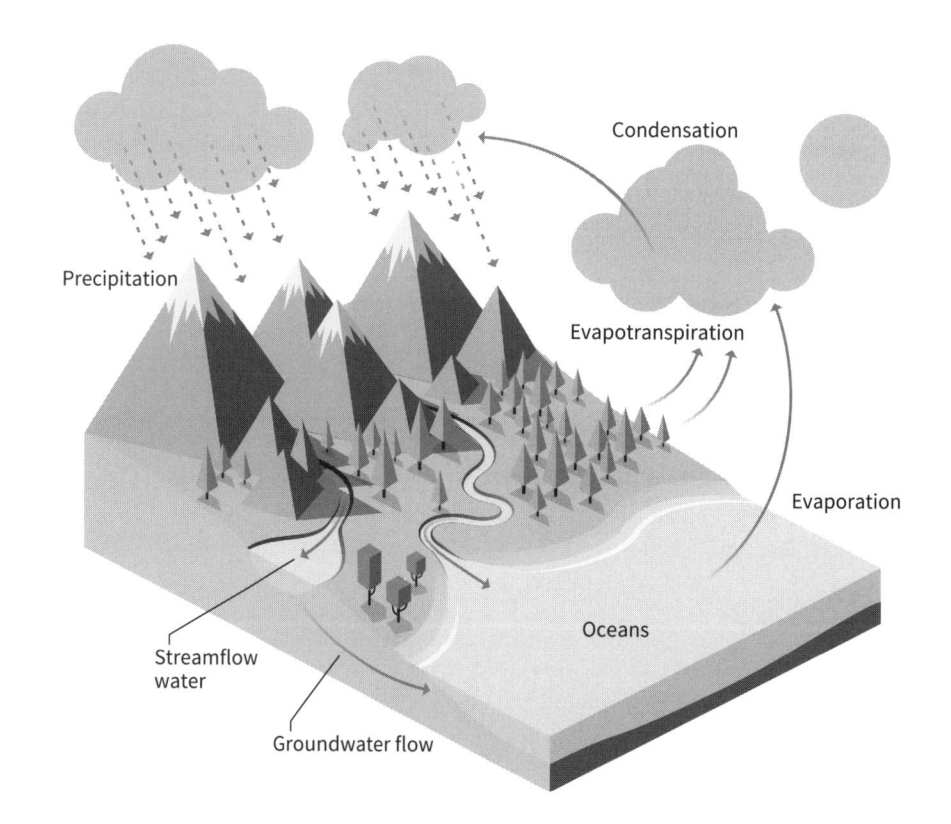

2.4 The water cycle

1   Write the names of the stages that are labelled **a** to **d** on the diagram.

    a   ....

    b   ....

    c   ....

    d   ....

Practice

2   Write the names of the stages that are labelled **e** to **g** on the diagram.

    e   ....

    f   ....

    g   ....

3   The process that takes place at **d** needs energy. Where does the energy come from?

    ....

4   Use particle theory to explain how water from the ocean reaches the clouds.

    ....

    ....

    ....

    ....

    ....

5   Explain why it rains.

    ....

    ....

    ....

    ....

2 Materials and their structure

Challenge

6 Explain what is meant by precipitation. What forms can precipitation take?

What conditions are needed for these different forms of precipitation to occur?

....

....

....

....

> 2.5 Atoms, elements and the Periodic Table

Exercise 2.5 Atoms, elements and the Periodic Table

This exercise will give you practice in using the symbols for elements and help you to remember facts about the Periodic Table.

Focus

1 Give the symbols for these elements.

　a　sodium ....

　b　magnesium ....

　c　boron ....

　d　calcium ....

　e　potassium ....

2.5 Atoms, elements and the Periodic Table

2 Give the names of the elements with these symbols.

a Ar .... c C .... e Li ....

b P .... d Cl ....

3 Scientists have organised all the elements into the Periodic Table.

Groups go up and down

Periods go across

a Complete this sentence:

The area shaded light grey contains elements that are

....

b Circle in red the **group** that contains the element magnesium.

c Circle in blue the **period** that contains the element oxygen.

Practice

4 Circle in green a group that contains both a metal and a non-metal.

5 Name a gas in the same period as carbon.

....

6 Name an element in the same group as calcium.

....

2 Materials and their structure

Challenge

7 Name an element that has atoms with a mass greater than those of aluminium.

   ....

8 Name an element that has atoms with a mass smaller than nitrogen but larger than beryllium.

   ....

> 2.6 Compounds and formulae

Exercise 2.6 Compounds and formulae

This exercise will help you to sort out facts about compounds and practise using formulae.

Focus

1 Write **true** or **false** next to each of these statements.

   a Each element is made of only one type of atom. ....

   b Oxygen is a compound. ....

   c Calcium is an element. ....

   d Water is an element. ....

   e This diagram shows an atom of sulfur.

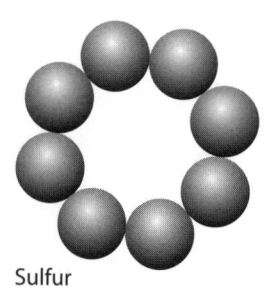

      ....

Sulfur

2.6 Compounds and formulae

f This diagram shows a compound of neon.

....

Neon

g A compound is made up of more than one type of atom.

....

2 a Which elements are in potassium chloride?

....

b Which is the metal in potassium chloride?

....

c Which elements are in magnesium oxide?

....

d Suggest the name of the compound that contains copper and oxygen.

....

e Suggest the name of the compound that contains iron and chlorine.

....

Practice

3 What is the name of the compound formed when these elements are combined together?

a sodium and oxygen ....

b calcium, carbon and oxygen ....

c potassium, nitrogen and oxygen ....

d potassium and nitrogen ....

e hydrogen and fluorine. ....

2 Materials and their structure

4 Which elements are found in these compounds?

a carbon dioxide ....

b copper sulfate ....

c aluminium chloride ....

d sodium sulfide ....

e calcium chlorate. ....

5 The formula for potassium hydroxide is KOH.
Which elements does it contain?

....

6 Complete this table.

Chemical name	Formula	What the compound contains
	MgO	
sulfur dioxide		one sulfur atom bonded to two oxygen atoms
aluminium chloride		one aluminium atom bonded to three chlorine atoms
calcium sulfide		one calcium atom bonded to one sulfur atom
	$MgCO_3$	

2.6 Compounds and formulae

Challenge

7 These formulae are written incorrectly. Rewrite them correctly.

a NA₂CO₃ ....

b CaCl2 ....

c CaCO³ ....

d O2 ....

e K₂Co₃ ....

8 a The formula for the sugar maltose is $C_{12}H_{22}O_{11}$.

What does this tell you about what the particle is made of?

....

....

b Suggest what $2C_{12}H_{22}O_{11}$ means.

....

9 a $Mg(OH)_2$ is the formula for which compound?

....

b How many oxygen atoms are there in this particle?

....

c How many hydrogen atoms are there in this particle?

....

10 Write the name and formula for a compound of calcium that contains oxygen and hydrogen atoms.

....

....

2 Materials and their structure

> 2.7 Compounds and mixtures

Exercise 2.7 Compounds and mixtures

This exercise helps you to distinguish (tell the difference) between mixtures and compounds.

Focus

In a compound, two or more elements are bonded together to make a new product.

In a mixture, two or more elements are mixed together, but they do not form a new product.

Marcus mixes iron filings and sulfur in a beaker. He stirs it until the two substances are completely mixed.

Sofia heats iron filings and sulfur powder together.

1 Tick (✓) **all** the correct statements.

    a Sofia produces a new product. ☐

    b Marcus produces a new product. ☐

    c Iron is magnetic. ☐

    d Something in Marcus's beaker is attracted to a magnet. ☐

2.7 Compounds and mixtures

e At the end of Sofia's experiment, something in Sofia's test tube is attracted to a magnet. ☐

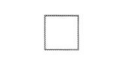

f At the end of Sofia's experiment the test tube contains a compound. ☐

g At the end of Marcus's experiment the beaker contains a compound. ☐

h At the end of the experiment the atoms in Marcus's beaker look like this. ☐

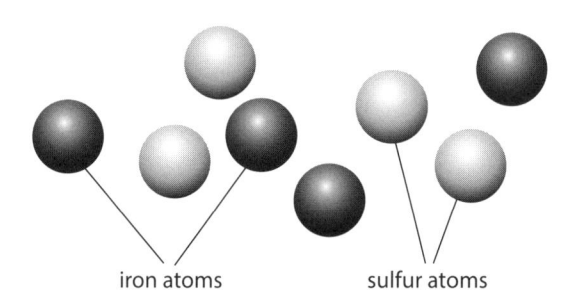

iron atoms   sulfur atoms

i At the end of the experiment the atoms in Sofia's test tube look like this. ☐

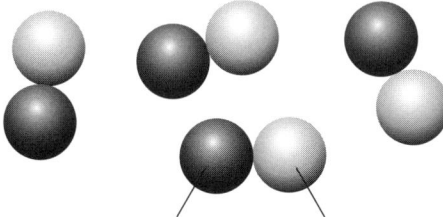

iron atom   sulfur atom

j Compounds have the same properties as the elements they are made from. ☐

2 Materials and their structure

Practice

Look at these particle diagrams.

Use the diagrams to answer the questions.

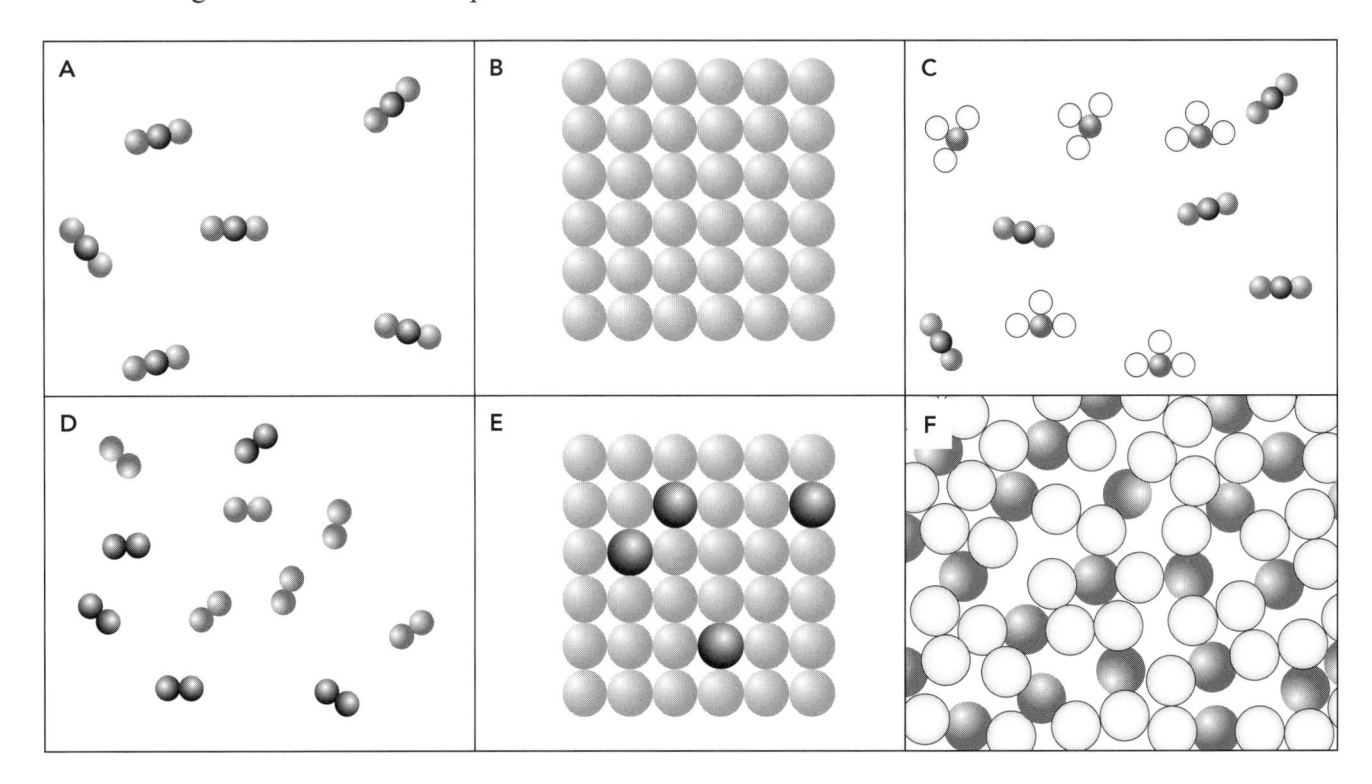

| A | B | C |
| D | E | F |

2 Which boxes contain gases?

....

3 Which boxes contain a mixture?

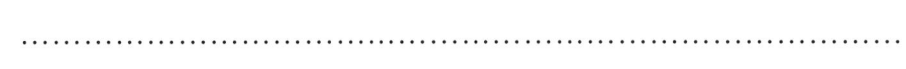

....

4 Which box contains a liquid?

....

2.7 Compounds and mixtures

Challenge

5 Which box contains a mixture of elements?

....

6 Which box contains a mixture of compounds?

....

7 a Give an example of a compound made from two elements and an example of a mixture of the same two elements.

....

....

b Explain the difference between a compound made of two elements and a mixture of the same two elements.

....

....

....

c Explain how the properties of the compound are different from the properties of the two elements.

....

....

....

d Explain how the properties of the mixture are different from those of the compound.

....

....

....

3 Forces and energy

> 3.1 Gravity, weight and mass

Exercise 3.1A Differences between weight and mass

Focus

This exercise will help you think about the differences between weight and mass.

1   Use the letters from the list to complete the sentences.

   g   kg   m   N

   Mass can be measured in …………………… or ……………………

   Weight is measured in………………………

2   Draw straight lines to match each description to the property it describes.

Description	Property
This is the force of gravity on an object.	
This is the quantity of matter in an object.	weight
This is constant, even when the strength of gravity changes.	mass
This changes, depending on the strength of gravity.	

3 The equation for working out the weight of an object on Earth is:

weight in N = mass in kg × 10 N/kg

Calculate the weight of each object.

Show your working and give the unit.

a A person of mass 75 kg

....

....

....

b A car of mass 900 kg

....

....

....

c An apple with a mass of 0.1 kg

....

....

....

3 Forces and energy

Exercise 3.1B Values of weight and mass

Practice

In this exercise you will be thinking about the values of weight and mass.

1   Look at this table.

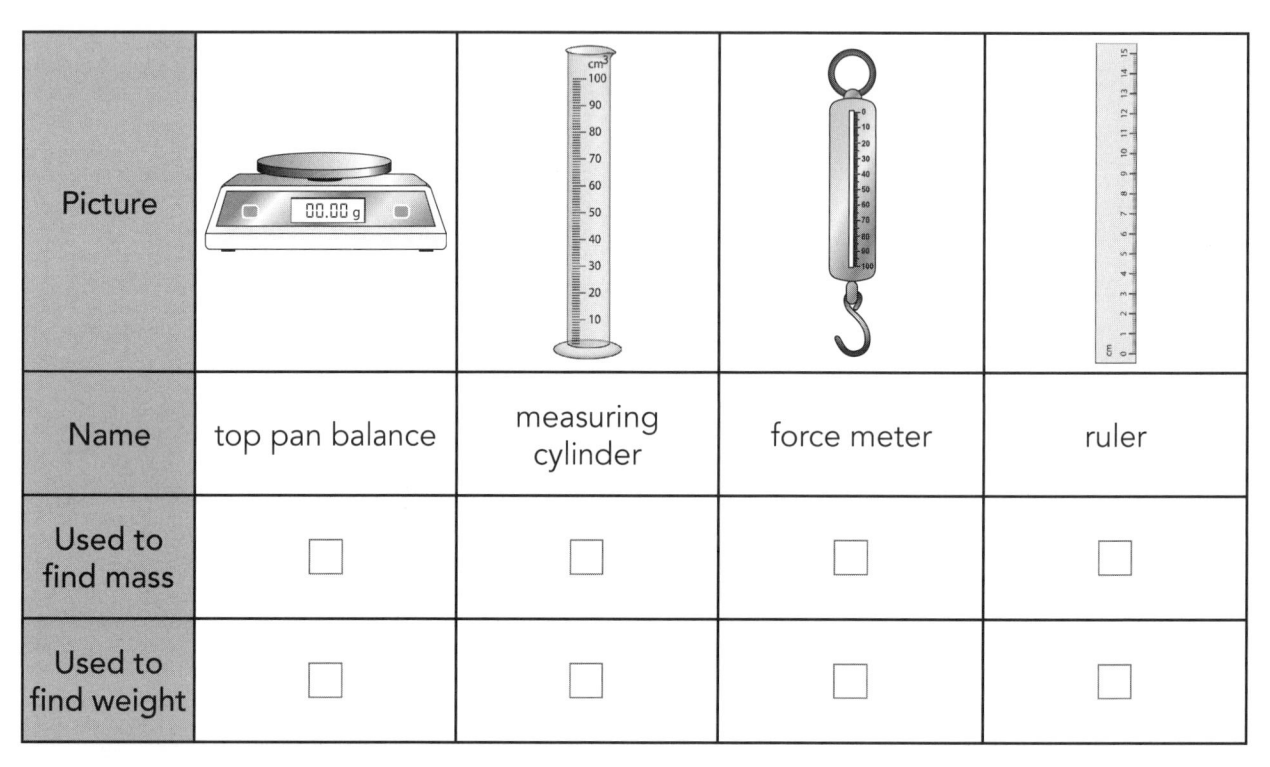

Picture				
Name	top pan balance	measuring cylinder	force meter	ruler
Used to find mass	☐	☐	☐	☐
Used to find weight	☐	☐	☐	☐

Tick (✓) one box in each row of the table to show which piece of equipment can be used to find the mass or the weight of an object.

2   Draw a circle around each of the values in this list that is a mass.

120 kg   1.5 N   4.91 m   6.04 kg   0.001 g   650 kN   975 mm

3.1 Gravity, weight and mass

3 The equation to calculate weight from mass on Earth is:

weight in N = mass in kg × 10 N/kg

   a   Calculate the mass of a box that has a weight of 250 N.

       Show your working and give the unit.

       ....

       ....

       ....

   b   Calculate the mass of a banana that has a weight of 0.9 N.

       Show your working and give the unit.

       ....

       ....

       ....

   c   Objects on the planet Mars have less weight than on Earth.

       The strength of gravity on Earth is given the value 10.

       Based on the two statements above, which of these is correct about the strength of gravity on Mars?

       Draw a circle around the correct answer.

It will also be 10.	It will be less than 10.	It will be greater than 10.	It is not possible to predict.

   d   Explain how the mass of an object on Mars would compare with the mass of the same object on Earth.

       ....

       ....

3 Forces and energy

Exercise 3.1C Effect of gravity on objects

Challenge

In this exercise you will consider the effect of gravity on objects.

1   The diagram represents the Earth. The direction in which gravity acts is shown with an arrow at point **A**.

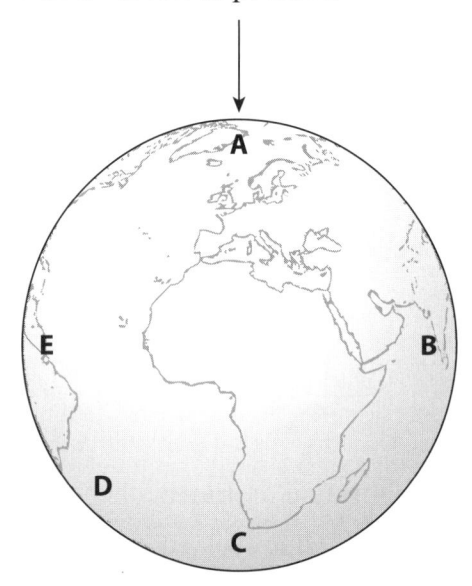

Draw arrows on the diagram to show the direction in which gravity acts at points **B**, **C**, **D** and **E**.

2   The force of gravity between two masses can be compared with the magnetic force between two magnets.

   a   Describe **two** ways that these forces are similar.

   1   ....

   ....

   2   ....

   ....

   b   Describe **one** way that these forces are different.

   ....

   ....

3.1 Gravity, weight and mass

3 Zara is investigating weight and mass.

She hangs masses on a piece of equipment that has a scale in newtons, N.

a Name the piece of equipment that Zara uses.

....

b Zara records the results in this table.

mass in kg	weight in N
0.1	1.0
0.2	2.0
0.3	2.9
0.4	3.9
0.5	4.9
0.6	5.9
0.7	6.8
0.8	7.8
0.9	8.8
1.0	9.8

Plot a graph of Zara's results on this grid. Put *mass in kg* along the horizontal axis and *weight in N* on the vertical axis.

c Complete the graph with a straight line of best fit.

d State the independent and dependent variables in this investigation.

Independent variable: ....

Dependent variable: ....

e Predict the weight of a 2.0 kg mass using Zara's results.

Show how you worked out your answer.

Give your answer to one decimal place and include the unit.

....

....

> 3.2 Formation of the Solar System

Exercise 3.2A Ideas about formation of the Solar System

Focus

In this exercise you will recall some facts about the Solar System.

1 The diagram shows the orbits of the planets around the Sun.

The direction of the orbit of Mercury is shown with an arrow.

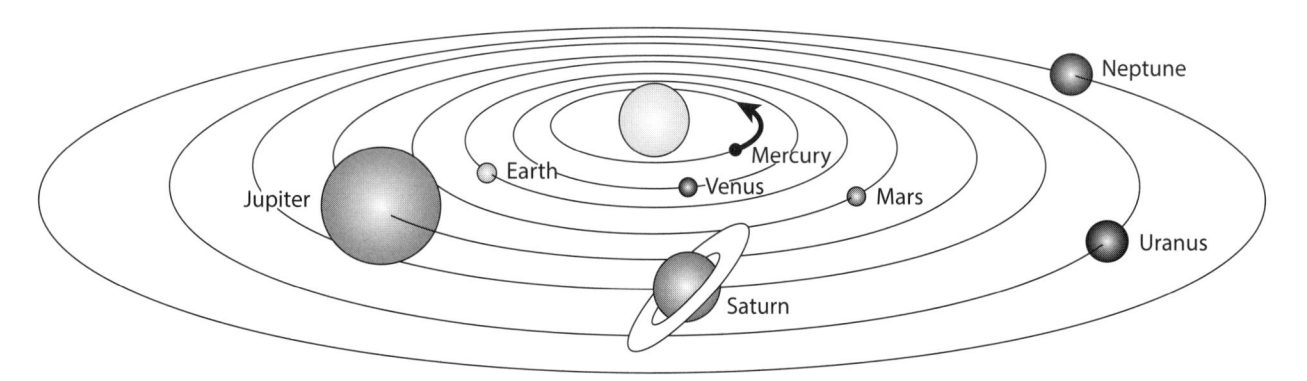

Draw arrows on the orbits of the other planets to show the direction that they move.

3.1 Gravity, weight and mass

2   a   Read this statement.

>   Scientists think that the Solar System formed from a cloud of dust and gas.

Which word describes this statement?
Underline the correct answer.

measurement   hypothesis   investigation   observation

b   Name the force that pulls particles of dust and gas together in space.

    ....

c   Scientists did not see the Solar System forming.

Complete the following sentence using a word from the list.

model   conclude   test   measure

Scientists use computers to .... the formation of the Solar System.

Exercise 3.2B Watching stars being born

Practice

In this exercise you will think about how scientists work.

There are some clouds of dust and gas in space that can be seen from Earth.

1   Write the name for a cloud of dust and gas in space.

    ....

3 Forces and energy

Scientists can see stars forming in the clouds of dust and gas in space.

2   Which piece of equipment helps the scientists to see the stars forming more clearly? Underline the correct answer.

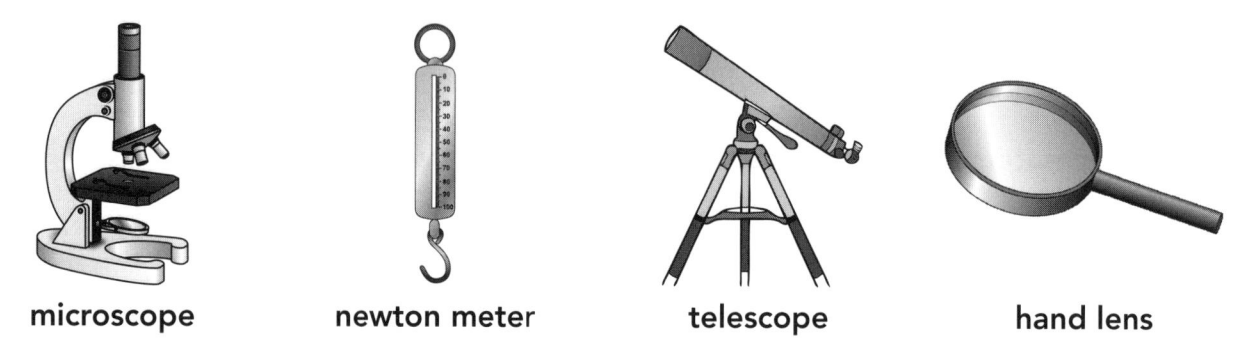

   microscope   newton meter   telescope   hand lens

3   When scientists see stars forming, what is this called?
    Underline the correct answer.

   an observation   a prediction   a conclusion   a measurement

4   Scientists can compare stars forming in different clouds of dust and gas at different places in space.

   When comparing the stars, which of these **cannot** be made?
   Underline the correct answer.

   observations   fair tests   conclusions   predictions

Exercise 3.2C Observing and predicting

Challenge

In this exercise you will think more about how scientists work.

Scientists think that the Solar System was formed from a cloud of dust and gas.

The Solar System took millions of years to form.

Scientists can see that stars are forming in clouds of dust and gas that are visible from Earth.

1   Explain why scientists **cannot** watch the complete process of a star and planets forming.

   ....

   ....

50

3.1 Gravity, weight and mass

2 Draw straight lines from each statement about the formation of the Solar System to its correct description. Some statements may match more than one description.

Statement	Description
Scientists think the Solar System formed from a cloud of dust and gas	evidence
Scientists use computers to demonstrate the formation of the Solar System.	observing
Scientists can see that stars are forming in clouds of dust and gas in space.	hypothesis
Scientists know that all the planets orbit the Sun in the same direction.	modelling

3 Forces and energy

> 3.3 Movement in Space

Exercise 3.3A Travelling through space

Focus

In this exercise you will recall some facts about how objects move in space.

1 The diagram shows a planet in orbit around the Sun.

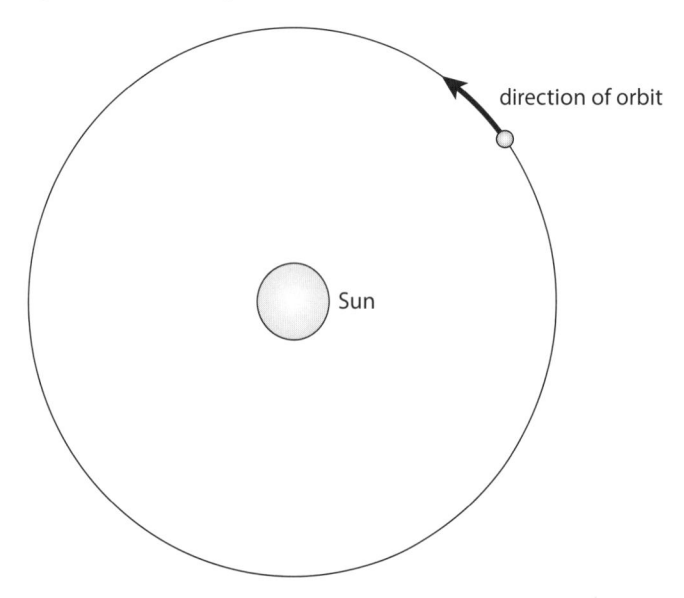

Draw an arrow on the diagram to show the direction of the force of the Sun's gravity on the planet.

2 A spacecraft is travelling from the Moon to Earth.

The space between the Moon and Earth contains no particles.

a Choose the name given to a space that contains no particles.

Underline the correct answer.

        gas   solid   vacuum   liquid

b What is the force that acts to slow the spacecraft in the air around Earth, but does **not** act on the spacecraft in space?

Underline the correct answer.

        gravity   air resistance   weight   pull

Exercise 3.3B Are there forces in space?

Practice

In this exercise you will think about what affects movement in space.

1 Some spacecraft were launched from Earth between the years 1972 and 1977.

   They were designed to take photographs of the planets.

   These spacecraft are now far outside the Solar System.

   These spacecraft do not have engines, but they are moving at a constant speed.

   Why are they able to move at a constant speed?

   Underline the correct answer.

   They have no mass.   There is no air resistance.

   They have no energy.   They have no weight.

2 The planet Saturn has rings.

   These rings are made from millions of separate pieces of rock. These pieces of rock are in orbit around Saturn.

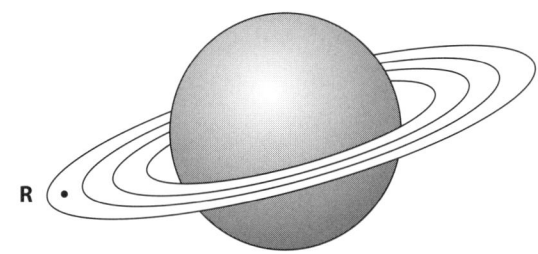

   A piece of rock in the rings is shown with the letter **R**.

   Draw an arrow to show the direction of the force that keeps **R** in orbit around Saturn.

3 Forces and energy

Exercise 3.3C Speeding up, slowing down and changing direction

Challenge

In this exercise you can demonstrate deeper understanding of how objects move in space.

1   The Space Shuttle was a type of spacecraft designed to take people into space.

    It was launched on a rocket with very powerful engines.

    a   Explain why very powerful engines are needed to go from Earth into space.

    ....

    ....

    In space, the speed of the Space Shuttle was about 28 000 km/h.

    When the Space Shuttle came back to Earth, its speed decreased very suddenly to about 300 km/h.

    Most of the force for slowing the Space Shuttle did **not** come from engines.

    b   Describe how the Space Shuttle was able to slow down so much **without** engines.

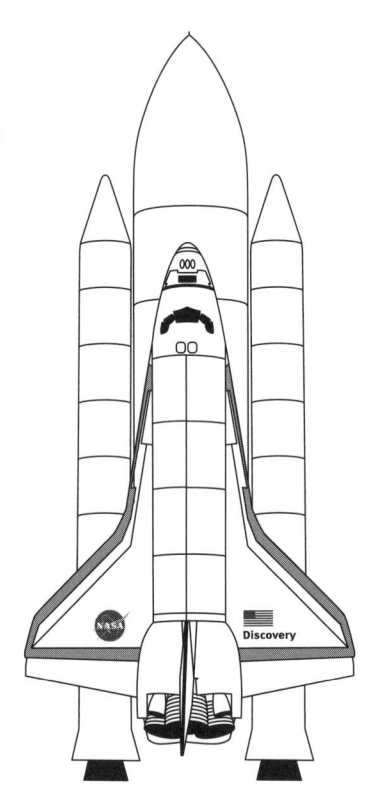

    ....

    ....

2   Voyager 2 was a spacecraft that was launched from Earth.

Voyager 2 passed close by Jupiter to take pictures. After passing Jupiter, Voyager 2 then continued its journey to Saturn.

The diagram shows the path of Voyager 2 towards Jupiter.

Voyager 2 did **not** have engines.

path of Voyager 2 →

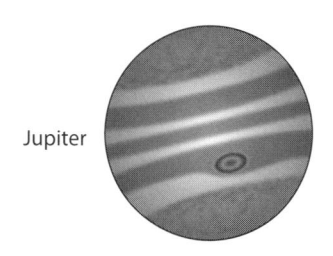

Jupiter

Continue the arrow to show how Voyager 2 passed Jupiter.
You can assume that Jupiter is **not** moving.

> 3.4 Tides

Exercise 3.4A High and low tides

Focus

In this exercise you will recall some facts about tides and what causes them.

1   Which of these causes high and low tides to happen on Earth?

Underline the correct answer.

air resistance   gravity from the planets only   tidal forces from the Sun only

tidal forces from the Sun and Moon

2   It is high tide in a harbour.

a   Write the number of hours until the next high tide in the same harbour..........................

b   Write the number of hours until the next low tide in the same harbour..........................

3 Forces and energy

3 Which of these positions of the Earth, the Moon and the Sun will cause the highest tides on Earth?

Tick (✓) **two** boxes.

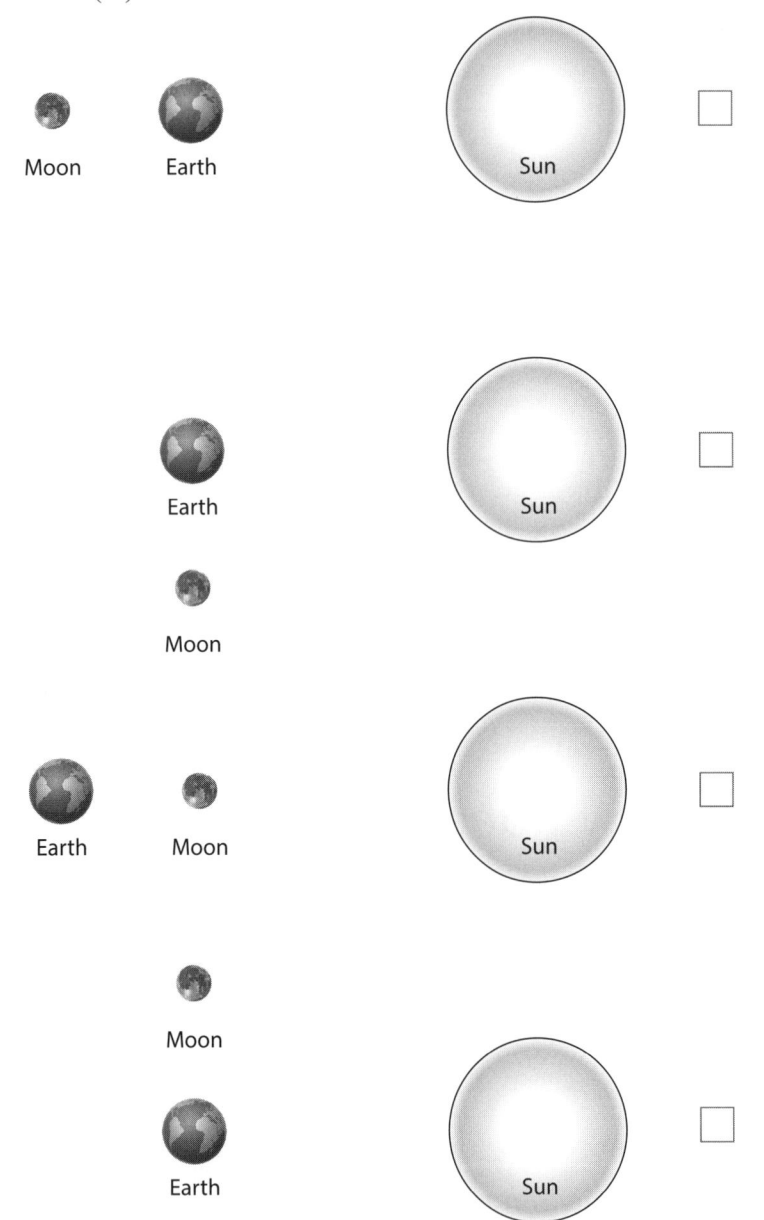

Moon   Earth   Sun   ☐

Earth   Sun   ☐

Moon

Earth   Moon   Sun   ☐

Moon

Earth   Sun   ☐

The diagrams are not to scale.

Exercise 3.4B Times of the tides

Practice

In this exercise you will think about the times of the tides.

1 It is high tide in a harbour at 05:00, when a boat goes out.

The boat cannot use the harbour at low tide.

At what times can the boat **not** get back into the harbour?

Underline the correct answer.

    11:00 same day   17:00 same day   05:00 next day   17:00 next day

2 Marcus is investigating tides at a harbour.

The harbour has a scale to measure the depth of water.

The scale is shown in the picture.

a State the depth of water shown in the picture.

……………………… m

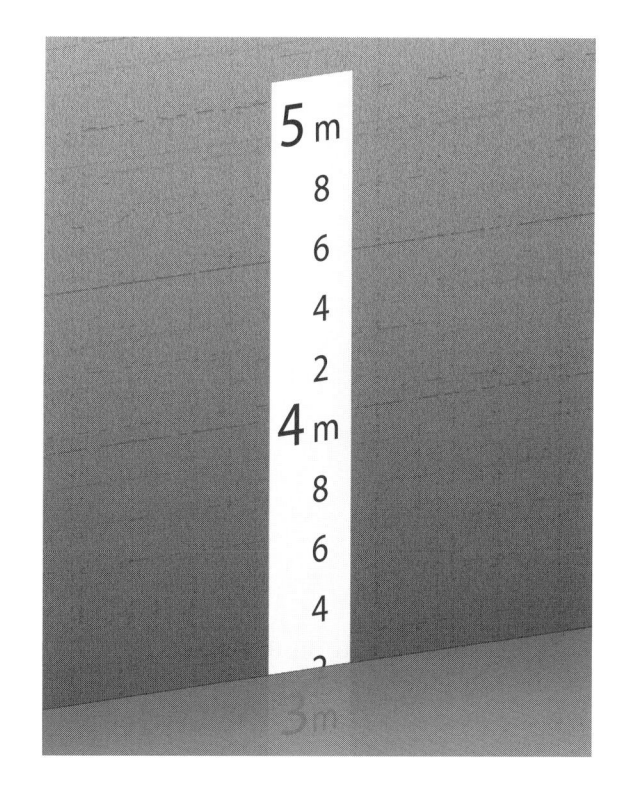

b Marcus wants to record how the depth of water in the harbour changes between one high tide and the next high tide.

Suggest a suitable time interval between the depth measurements.

…………………………………………………………………………………………

3 Forces and energy

Exercise 3.4C Forces and tides

Challenge

In this exercise you will think about the forces causing the tides.

The Moon's gravity causes tides on Earth.

1   A force caused by gravity from the Moon makes the tides.

   Complete the sentence using the best word.

   This force is called a ……………………… force.

2   The diagram shows the Moon and Earth.

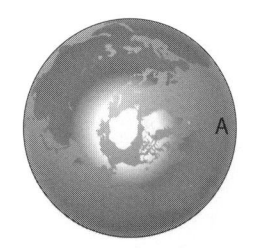

   Earth   Moon

   Draw an arrow to show the direction of the force which causes tides at position **A** on Earth.

3   Explain whether position **A** has a high tide or a low tide.

   ………………………………………………………………………………..

   ………………………………………………………………………………..

4   The time at position **A** is now 08:00.

   Give the time of the next tide of the same type at position A.

   ………………………

> 3.5 Energy

Exercise 3.5A Describing energy

Focus

In this exercise you will recall the descriptions of energy.

Draw straight lines to match the energy store or transfer to its description.

Energy	Description
elastic	energy stored in hot objects
gravitational potential	energy transferred by current in wires
electrical	energy stored in fuel
chemical	energy in objects that are lifted higher
sound	energy that we can see
thermal	energy stored in an object that has changed shape
light	energy of moving objects
kinetic	energy transferred from vibrations

3 Forces and energy

Exercise 3.5B Examples of energy

Practice

In this exercise you will describe examples of energy.

1 Complete the sentences. Use the correct words for the energy in each sentence.

   a Food is a store of ………………… energy.

   b A book lifted up onto a shelf has a store of
      ……………… energy.

   c The Sun transfers ……………… energy and
      ……………… energy to Earth.

   d A musical instrument transfers ……………… energy to our ears.

2 A fire is burning wood for cooking.

   The fire is 20 cm above the ground.

   A piece of wood that is still burning is falling out of the fire.

   The piece of burning wood has fallen through 10 cm.

   Tick (✓) the boxes to show how energy is either stored or transferred by the wood.

Energy	Stored	Transferred
gravitational potential	☐	☐
elastic	☐	☐
electrical	☐	☐
thermal	☐	☐
light	☐	☐
chemical	☐	☐

Exercise 3.5C Energy investigations

Challenge

In this exercise you will think about how scientists work.

A waterfall is where water drops down steeply or vertically.

1 Name the energy that the water gains as it falls faster down the waterfall.

   ....

3 Forces and energy

2 In the year 1847 two scientists, named James Joule and William Thomson (later to be Lord Kelvin), visited a waterfall.

Joule: I think the temperature of the water at the bottom of the waterfall will be higher than at the top.

Kelvin: Let's go and find out!

Joule

Kelvin

What sort of statement is Joule making?

Underline the correct answer.

an observation   a prediction   a measurement   a conclusion

3 Joule and Kelvin tried to measure the temperature of the water at the top and at the bottom of the waterfall. The waterfall was over 200 m high.

Joule and Kelvin did **not** complete their investigation because it was too difficult.

We now know that the temperature difference between the top and bottom of the waterfall is less than 1 °C.

Suggest **two** reasons why this investigation was too difficult for them.

1 ....

....

2 ....

....

> 3.6 Changes in Energy

Exercise 3.6A Energy diagrams

Focus

In this exercise you will complete some energy diagrams.

Complete the energy diagrams to show the energy changes in each of these processes.

The first one has been done for you.

	Process	Burning gas for heating
	Diagram	chemical → thermal

		Process	Using an electric lamp
1		Diagram	electrical → ⬚

		Process	Using a music player
2		Diagram	electrical → ⬚

		Process	A gasoline (petrol) engine driving a car
3		Diagram	⬚ → kinetic

		Process	Dropping a ball
4		Diagram	⬚ → ⬚

3 Forces and energy

Exercise 3.6B Reading from a graph

Practice

In this exercise you will use a graph to answer questions about energy transfer.

The graph shows how the temperature of water changes when thermal energy is transferred to the water.

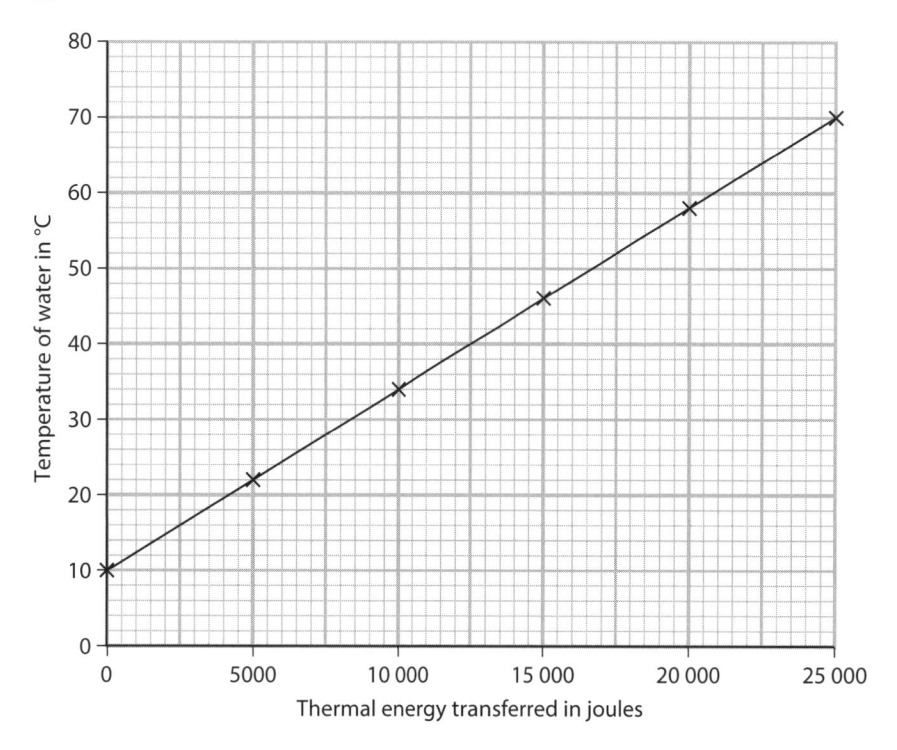

1   Complete the sentence using the words **increases** or **decreases**.

   As the thermal energy transferred .... ,

   the temperature of the water ....

2   Write down the temperature of the water when no additional thermal energy had been transferred.

   .... °C

3   Write down the quantity of thermal energy that was needed to change the temperature of the water from 10 °C to 70 °C.

   Show on the graph how you worked out the answer.

   .... J

64

3.6 Changes in Energy

4 Which of these must remain constant during this investigation?

Underline the correct answer.

temperature of the water   thermal energy supplied

mass of water used   thermometer that was used

Exercise 3.6C Series of energy changes

Challenge

In this exercise you will describe a series of energy changes.

The picture shows a jumping toy.

When the toy is pushed down, a spring inside the toy is squeezed tight.

When the toy is released, it jumps up from the surface.

It reaches a height of about 20 cm before it falls down again. It does not jump again until pushed.

Describe the energy changes that happen in this toy.

- Start your description when the toy is pushed down.
- Include the energy change in the jump.
- End your description when the toy comes down onto the surface.

....

....

....

....

....

....

....

3 Forces and energy

> 3.7 Where does energy go?

Exercise 3.7A Energy wordsearch

Focus

In this exercise you will recall some words about where energy goes, and their spellings.

Answer the clues, then find the word in the wordsearch. The first one has been done for you.

The words may read horizontally or vertically, backwards or forwards.

E	D	E	S	T	R	O	Y	E	D	D	T	D	T
U	E	D	E	T	S	A	W	W	I	W	D	E	L
D	G	U	E	A	E	Y	U	L	I	T	S	T	I
S	S	E	T	S	F	A	S	U	L	H	L	A	G
T	R	E	G	R	E	E	P	F	S	E	W	P	H
O	E	D	L	A	T	I	D	E	R	R	N	I	T
R	A	R	S	A	N	E	Y	S	A	M	D	S	U
E	I	S	H	S	S	I	E	U	T	A	O	S	E
D	R	E	C	O	V	E	R	E	D	L	T	I	U
N	C	L	S	F	D	N	U	O	S	E	D	D	E
I	E	E	L	I	R	U	G	O	R	R	W	S	E
D	O	E	N	E	R	G	Y	D	E	W	D	E	D
S	E	S	E	U	E	E	D	R	H	T	I	T	H
E	U	D	O	T	D	A	R	F	G	D	G	U	S

Clues

1 ENERGY must be transferred to make something happen.
   (6 letters, starts with E)

2 Energy that can be kept for a long time is .... energy. (6 letters, starts with S)

3 Energy that we want is called .... energy.
   (6 letters, starts with U)

4 Energy that we do not want is called .... energy.
  (6 letters, starts with W)

5 Energy that is wasted cannot be ....
  (9 letters, starts with R)

6 Energy that spreads out and becomes less useful has

  .... (10 letters, starts with D)

7 Three transfers of energy that spread out and cannot be used again are:

  .... (5 letters, starts with L)

  .... (7 letters, starts with T)

  .... (5 letters, starts with S)

8 Although energy can be wasted, it can never be

  .... (9 letters, starts with D)

Exercise 3.7B Energy loss

Practice

In this exercise, you will think about investigating energy loss.

Zara wants to measure how the temperature of hot water changes with time.

She sets up three beakers of hot water.

The temperatures of the water in the beakers at the start are:
- 50 °C
- 70 °C
- 90 °C

Zara then records the temperature in each beaker every minute.

1 List two variables that must be kept constant when comparing the beakers.

  1 ....

  2 ....

3 Forces and energy

The temperature of the water in each of the beakers decreases.

2 Name the energy that is lost from the water.

   ....

3 List two places that this energy will go to when it leaves the water.

   1 ....

   2 ....

4 Describe how you could demonstrate that the energy had gone where you predicted.

   ....

   ....

   ....

   ....

5 Zara follows the usual safety rules for a science laboratory.

   Describe **one more** safety precaution needed in this investigation.

   ....

   ....

Exercise 3.7C Wasted energy

Challenge

In this exercise you will think about the stores and quantities of energy that are wasted.

1 A machine transfers 80% of the energy it uses to wasted energy.

   Calculate the percentage of **useful** energy transferred by the machine.

   Show your working.

   ....

2 A gasoline (petrol) engine in a car transfers 25% of the energy it uses to useful energy.

    a Calculate the percentage of the energy that is transferred to wasted energy.

       Show your working.

       .... %

    b Suggest two ways that energy is wasted by the car engine.

       ....

       ....

    c A diesel engine in a large truck transfers 30% of the energy it uses to useful energy.

       A diesel engine is more expensive than a gasoline engine of the same size.

       Suggest why diesel engines are used instead of gasoline engines in large trucks.

       Think about:
- what large trucks are used for
- the length of time large trucks are travelling
- the money spent on fuel.

....

....

....

....

....

....

4 Grouping and identifying organisms

4.1 Characteristics of living organisms

Exercise 4.1A Matching terms and descriptions

Focus

This exercise on the next page will help you to check that you understand the seven characteristics of living organisms.

4.1 Characteristics of living organisms

The boxes on the left of the diagram show the seven characteristics of living organisms.

The boxes on the right show descriptions of each characteristic.

Draw **one** straight line from each characteristic to its description.

Characteristic	Description
nutrition	getting bigger
respiration	detecting changes in the environment
excretion	making new individuals of the same kind of organism
reproduction	feeding – taking in materials from the environment for energy and growth
growth	changing the position of part or all of the body
sensitivity	breaking down nutrients to release energy
movement	getting rid of waste materials

4 Grouping and identifying organisms

Exercise 4.1B Characteristics of living organisms wordsearch

Practice

In this exercise you will learn and remember the seven characteristics of living organisms, and how to spell them.

Answer the clues, then find the word in the wordsearch. The words may read horizontally, vertically or diagonally, backwards or forwards. The first one has been done for you.

Z	Q	X	U	E	E	B	C	Y	S	T	N	P	R
R	A	C	H	P	X	E	L	H	T	W	O	R	G
E	M	Q	U	A	L	W	H	T	R	E	I	N	E
S	J	U	Z	C	K	E	M	N	I	X	T	F	S
P	G	N	W	Y	A	O	O	M	T	C	C	X	E
I	M	P	C	B	L	I	V	K	D	R	U	S	T
R	H	C	T	I	T	O	E	C	E	E	D	R	L
A	U	P	B	I	E	I	M	O	U	T	O	W	T
T	E	R	R	V	S	C	E	P	S	I	R	R	E
I	N	T	R	E	S	K	N	F	F	O	P	E	R
O	U	Y	T	I	V	I	T	I	S	N	E	S	G
N	H	I	J	T	U	F	V	J	E	A	R	D	E

Clues

1 Being able to sense and respond to stimuli. ......Sensitivity......

2 A chemical reaction that takes place in all living cells, releasing energy from food. ....

3 Changing the position or shape of part of the body.

   ....

4   Getting rid of waste products from the chemical reactions taking place inside body cells. ....

5   Taking in nutrients that are needed to keep the organism alive.

    ....

6   Making new living organisms. ....

7   A permanent increase in size. ....

Exercise 4.1C Living or not?

Challenge

In this exercise, you will have to think hard about what makes something alive.

An elephant, an apple and a seed are all living organisms.

Do you think that all living organisms show all of the characteristics of living organisms all of the time?

Use the elephant, apple and seed to explain your answer.

....

....

....

....

....

....

....

....

....

4 Grouping and identifying organisms

> 4.2 Viruses

Exercise 4.2 All about viruses

Focus

1   Complete the sentences about viruses.

    Choose from the words in the list. You may use each word once, more than once or not at all.

    big   cells   move   protein   replicate   small

    Viruses are very ………………………… . Viruses are not made of

    ………………………… . Viruses can only …………………… when

    they are inside a living cell.

Practice

2   Scientists do not all agree about whether viruses are living organisms.

    A: Viruses are living organisms.

    B: I do not agree that viruses should be classed as living organisms.

4.2 Viruses

   a   Write down **one** piece of information about viruses that
       supports the view of Scientist **A**.

       ....

       ....

   b   Write down **two** pieces of information about viruses that
       support the view of Scientist **B**.

       ....

       ....

       ....

Challenge

3 Viruses were first discovered in 1892.

   Use the internet to find out how this discovery happened.

   a   Which websites did you use? Explain why you decided that
       these websites provided reliable information, and were not
       biased or scientifically incorrect.

       ....

       ....

       ....

       ....

       ....

       ....

b Use your own words to write a short description of how viruses were first discovered.

....

....

....

....

....

....

....

> 4.3 What is a species?

Exercise 4.3A Different species

Focus

This exercise will help you to check that you understand what the term 'species' means.

Complete the sentences on the next page.

Choose from these words or phrases.

You can use each word or phrase once, more than once or not at all.

| different to | exactly the same as | fight | fertile | healthy |
| horn | horns | infertile | kingdoms | reproduce | species |

4.3 What is a species?

The drawings show a white rhinoceros and an Indian rhinoceros.

Indian rhinoceros

white rhinoceros

White rhinoceroses and Indian rhinoceroses belong to different .... This means that they cannot .... with each other to produce .... offspring.

White rhinoceroses and Indian rhinoceroses do not look .... one another. Indian rhinoceroses have one .... but white rhinoceroses have two ....

4 Grouping and identifying organisms

Exercise 4.3B Horses, donkeys and mules

Practice

This exercise is about the meaning of the word 'species'. It will also give you practice in observing carefully and recording your observations.

Donkeys and horses belong to different species.

People sometimes breed a female horse with a male donkey. The offspring is called a mule. Mules are big and strong, like horses. They are quiet and easy to handle, like donkeys. Mules are infertile.

horse

mule

donkey

1 Write down **three** similarities between a horse and a donkey.

First similarity:

....

....

Second similarity:

....

....

Third similarity:

....

....

2 Write down **two** ways in which a donkey differs from a horse.

   First difference:

   ....

   ....

   Second difference:

   ....

   ....

3 Find **two** pieces of evidence in the information at the start of this exercise to show that horses and donkeys belong to **different** species.

   First piece of evidence:

   ....

   ....

   Second piece of evidence:

   ....

   ....

4 Grouping and identifying organisms

Exercise 4.3C A new frog species

Challenge

In this task, you will use your understanding of what makes a separate species. You will suggest how scientists could decide how to classify a newly discovered kind of frog.

In 2016, a team of researchers from India and the National University of Singapore discovered an unusual frog in a rocky habitat near the coast of southwest India.

The frog is tiny – only about 16 mm long. It looks similar to other little frogs that are classified in the genus *Microhyla*. This frog is pale brown and has black and orangey-red markings on its back, feet and sides. The males make a call that sounds like a cricket chirping.

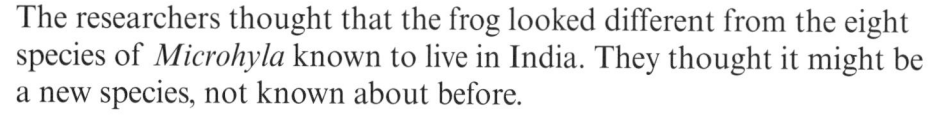

The researchers thought that the frog looked different from the eight species of *Microhyla* known to live in India. They thought it might be a new species, not known about before.

Suggest what the researchers should do to decide whether or not their frog really is a new species. You could think about these things.

- How many specimens of the new frog should they collect? (Think about how much evidence they need, as well as the fact that this species might be rare.)

- What evidence should the researchers collect in order to test the hypothesis that the new frog belongs to a new species?

- How should the researchers use this evidence to make a decision about whether or not the frog belongs to a new species?

- How might other scientists evaluate the evidence of these researchers, and continue the research to obtain more evidence?

....

....

....

....
....
....
....
....
....
....
....
....

> 4.4 Using keys

Exercise 4.4A Using a key to identify a fruit

Focus

This exercise gives you practice in using a key.

The diagrams show fruits from three different plants.

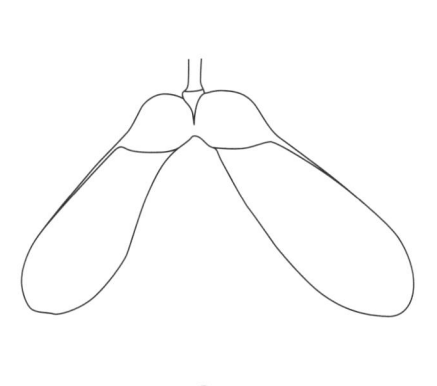

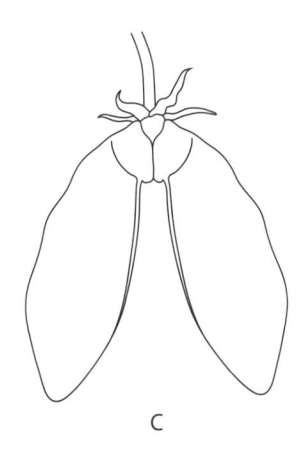

A B C

4 Grouping and identifying organisms

Use the key to identify fruit B.

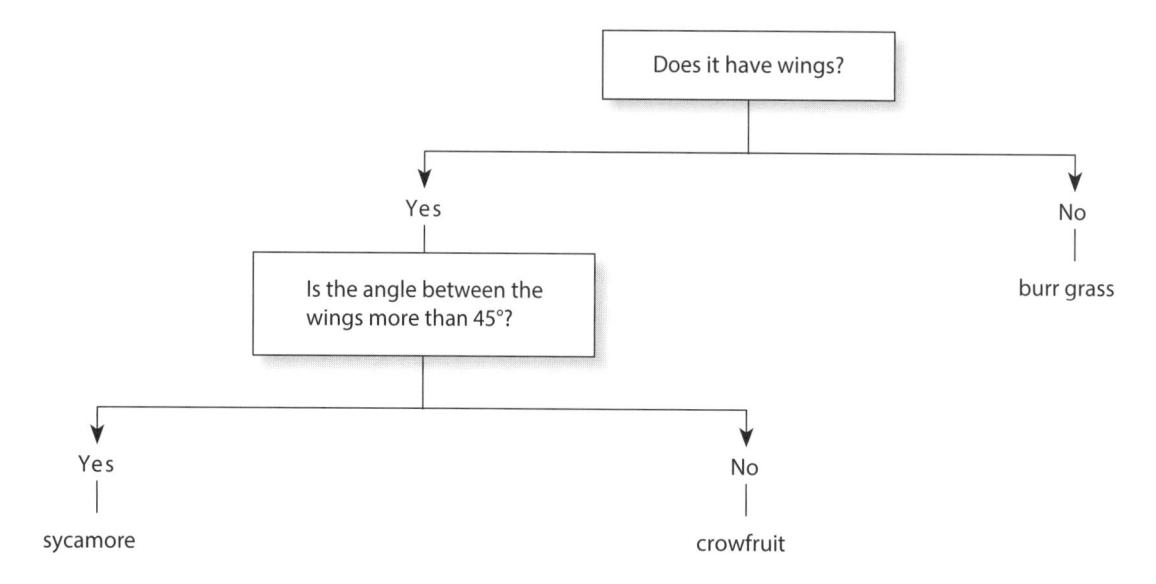

```
                    Does it have wings?
                   /                    \
                 Yes                     No
                  |                       |
    Is the angle between the          burr grass
    wings more than 45°?
        /            \
      Yes             No
       |               |
   sycamore         crowfruit
```

Fruit **B** is ………………………… .

4.4 Using keys

Exercise 4.4B Using a key to identify four fish

Practice

In this exercise, you will practise using a key consisting of paired statements.

The diagrams show four fish.

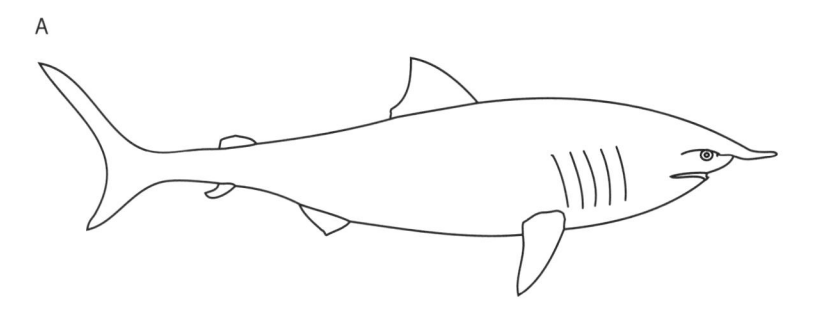

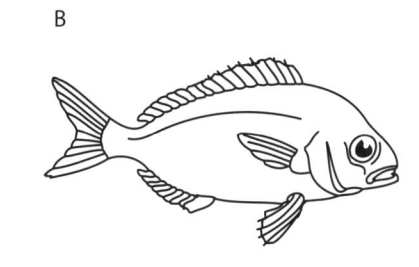

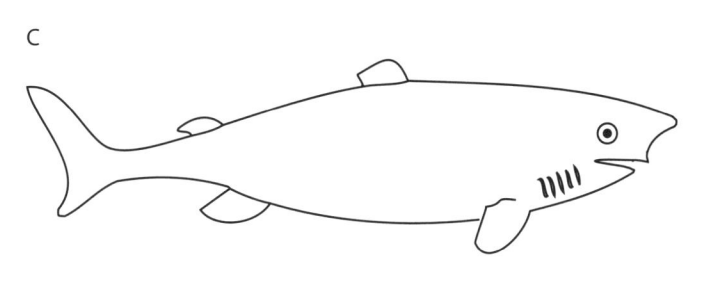

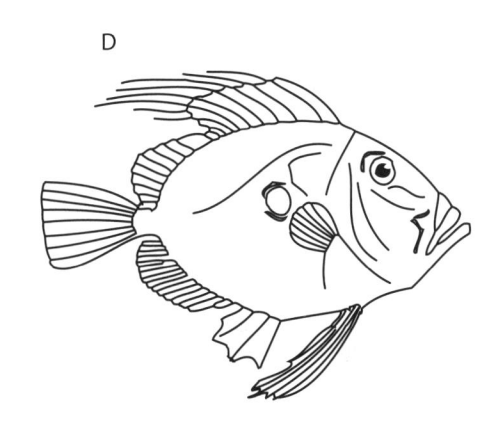

A

B

C

D

Key:			
1	a	It has a row of gill slits	go to step 2
	b	No gill slits can be seen	go to step 3
2	a	Its eye is above the front end of its mouth	**basking shark**
	b	Its eye is above the back end of its mouth	**Greenland shark**
3	a	It has long spines on its top fin	**John Dory**
	b	It has short spines on its top fin	**sea bream**

4 Grouping and identifying organisms

In the questions, you will use this key to find out the name of each fish.
Start with fish A.
Look at step **1** in the key. Read descriptions **1a** and **1b**.

1   a   Which description fits fish A? ....
        The key tells you which step to go to next.
        Go to this step, and choose which description fits fish A.

    b   What is the name of fish A? ....
        Now work through the key to identify fish B.

2   a   Which description in step 1 fits fish B? ....
        Go to the next step.

    b   What is the name of fish B? ....
        Now work through the key again to identify fish C.

3   What is the name of fish C?

    ....

4   Identify fish C.

    ....

84

4.4 Using keys

Exercise 4.4C Using a key to identify tree species from their leaves

Challenge

In this exercise, you will use a key to identify the species of tree from which each of these five leaves has been collected.

The photographs show five leaves.

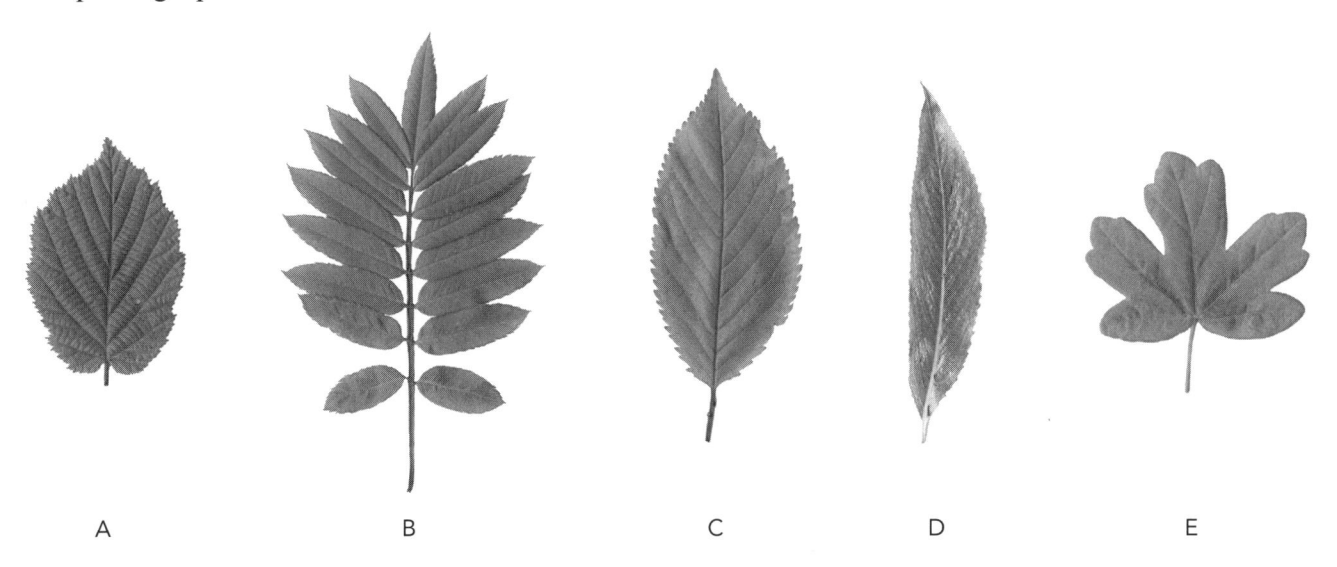

A B C D E

Key:			
1	a	leaf is made up of many small leaflets	**rowan**
	b	leaf is not made up of many small leaflets	go to 2
2	a	leaf is oval	go to 3
	b	leaf is not oval and has five lobes	**maple**
3	a	leaf is at least twice as long as it is wide	go to 4
	b	leaf is less than twice as long as it is wide	**hazel**
4	a	leaf has shiny surface	**willow**
	b	leaf has dull surface	**cherry**

1   Use the key to identify leaf A.

   Leaf A is ....

4 Grouping and identifying organisms

2 Write down the statements, in order, that led you to your answer.

   ....

   ....

   ....

3 Now identify each of the other leaves. Write down the statements, in order, that led you to each answer.

   ....

   ....

   ....

   ....

   ....

> 4.5 Writing keys

Exercise 4.5 Making a key to identify plant species from their leaves

In this task, you will first choose some features that help you to tell the difference between five leaves. Then you will try using some of these features to construct a key.

The pictures show leaves from five different plants.

potentilla   Solomon's seal   wisteria   mullein   plume thistle

Focus

1 Make a list of **three** features of the leaves that you can use to tell them apart.

   ....

   ....

   ....

   ....

Practice

2 Use some of your ideas in question 1 to write a key to help someone to identify these leaves.

   The first box has been drawn for you. Write a question in this box, and then add more questions in boxes until you have finished your key.

4 Grouping and identifying organisms

Remember that your key must work when the person has only one leaf, with no others to compare it with.

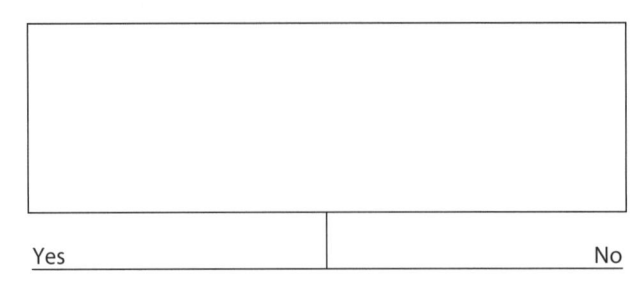

```
┌─────────────────────────────────┐
│                                 │
│                                 │
│                                 │
└────────────────┬────────────────┘
Yes                              No
```

Challenge

3   Write your key from Question **2** in the style that uses pairs of statements.

5 Properties of materials

> 5.1 Metals and non-metals

Exercise 5.1 Metal properties and uses

Focus

This exercise will help you to match properties of metals with their uses.

1　Look at the drawings. Use them to help you to complete the sentences.

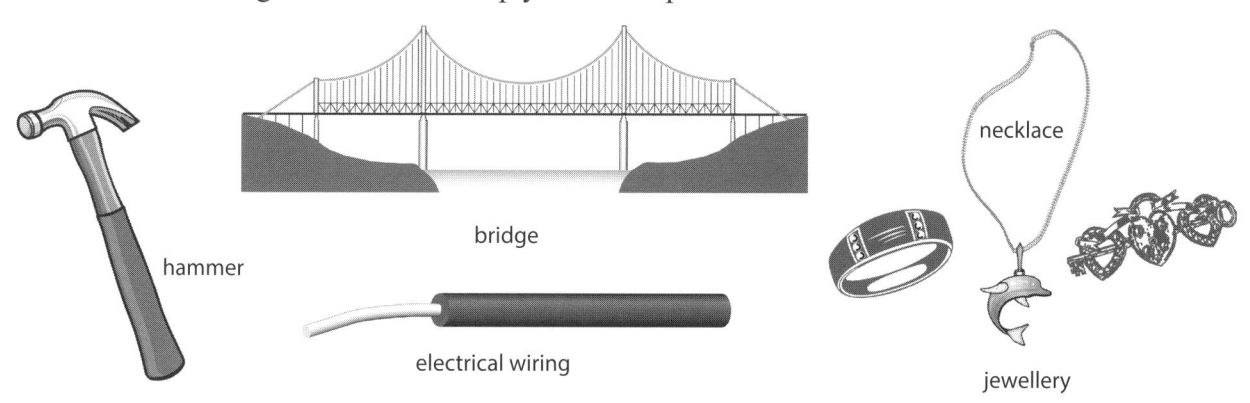

hammer

bridge

electrical wiring

necklace

jewellery

a　Metals are strong and tough.

　　This is why iron is used for ………………………………… .

b　Metals are usually shiny.

　　This is why gold is used for ………………………………… .

c　Metals are good conductors of electricity.

　　This is why copper is used for ………………………………… .

5 Properties of materials

2 Draw a circle around each word (or group of words) that describes a property of metals.

malleable   has a dull surface   does not conduct electricity

makes a ringing sound when tapped   ductile

feels cold to the touch   conducts heat   brittle   has a shiny surface

Practice

Doing this wordsearch will help you to learn and remember the properties of metals and how to spell them.

3 Find the words with these meanings.

- **a** Rings like a bell when hit ....
- **b** Can be pulled out into wires ....
- **c** Can be changed into different shapes ....
- **d** Is the opposite of dull ....
- **e** Is attracted to a magnet ....
- **f** Allows heat and electricity to pass through it ....
- **g** All the features of metals are their ....

Z	Q	X	U	E	E	B	C	Y	S	T	S	P	R
R	A	C	H	P	X	E	L	H	T	W	H	R	G
E	M	A	L	L	E	A	B	L	E	E	I	N	E
S	A	U	Z	C	K	S	M	N	I	X	N	F	S
P	G	D	W	Y	A	O	O	M	T	C	Y	X	E
I	N	U	C	B	L	N	V	K	D	R	U	S	T
R	E	C	T	P	R	O	P	E	R	T	I	E	S
A	T	T	B	I	E	R	M	O	U	T	O	W	T
T	I	I	R	V	C	O	N	D	U	C	T	O	R
I	C	L	R	E	S	U	N	F	F	O	P	E	R
O	U	E	T	I	V	S	T	R	O	N	G	S	G
N	H	I	J	T	U	F	V	J	E	A	R	D	E

5.1 Metals and non-metals

Challenge

4 Choose a metal, one that is used in your classroom or home, and write a careful description of it. Use the correct scientific terms. Explain which properties of metals are particularly suited to the function it has.

....

....

....

....

....

....

....

....

....

....

....

....

....

....

....

....

....

5 Properties of materials

> 5.2 Comparing metals and non-metals

Exercise 5.2A Metal or non-metal?

Focus

In this exercise, you will sort metals and non-metals and draw a bar chart.

Sofia has mixed up this list of metals and non-metals. She needs to sort them out.

1 Tick each answer in the table that Sofia has correct.

List of materials	Sofia's answer	Correct?
Silver	Metal	
Oxygen	Non-metal	
Helium	Non-metal	
Carbon	Metal	
Copper	Metal	
Nitrogen	Non-metal	
Sulfur	Metal	
Iron	Metal	

2 How many metals does Sofia think there are? ....

3 What is the correct number of metals? ....

4 How many non-metals does Sofia think there are?

....

5.2 Comparing metals and non-metals

5   What is the correct number of non-metals? ....

6   Use the correct numbers from questions 3 and 5 to complete and fully label the bar chart.

Use a pencil and ruler, but do not shade the bars.

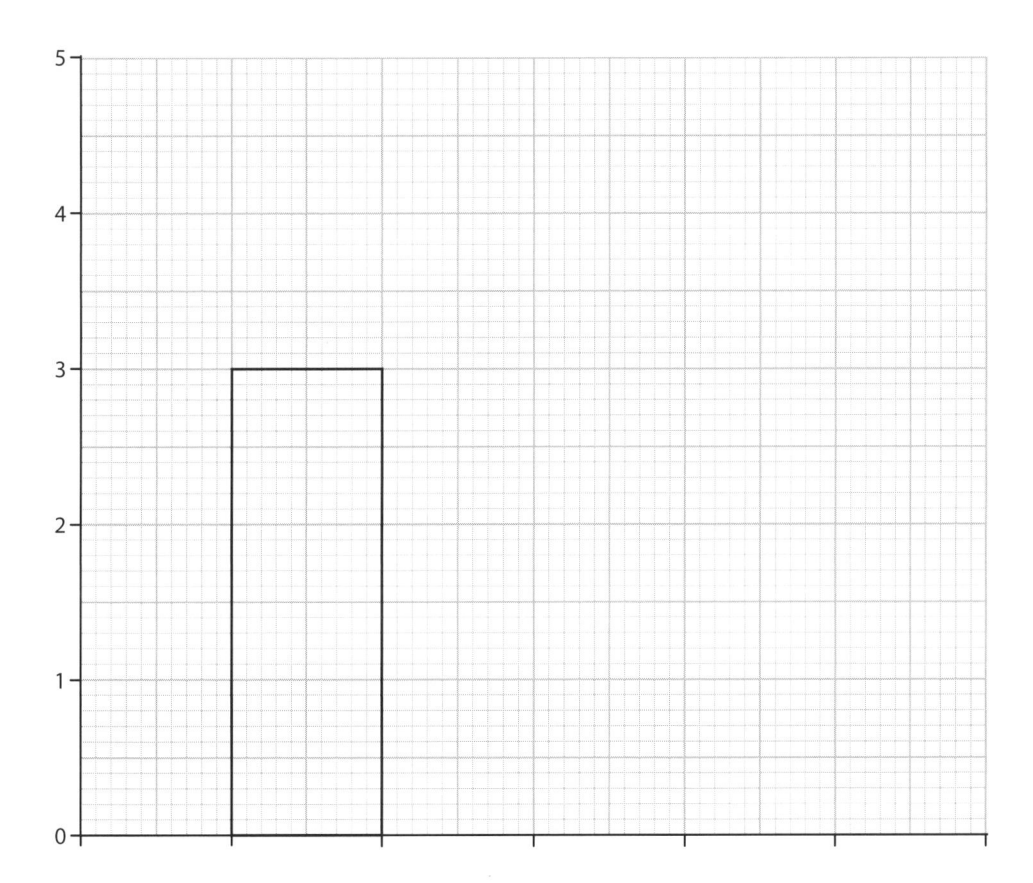

Exercise 5.2B Comparing metals and non-metals

Practice

This exercise will help you remember how to distinguish between metals and non-metals.

1   Draw a labelled diagram to show how you could test a material to find out if it conducts electricity or not.

2   Write 'true' or 'false' next to each of these statements.

   a   All metals are magnetic. ....

   b   Solid non-metals are brittle. ....

   c   All metals are solids. ....

   d   Metals conduct heat energy. ....

   e   Non-metals are good conductors of electricity.

       ....

5.2 Comparing metals and non-metals

Exercise 5.2C Identifying metals and non-metals

Challenge

In this exercise, you will try to identify substances from the information you are given.

Here is some information about six substances.

Substance A: This is a shiny liquid. The melting point is −39°C and the boiling point is 357°C. It conducts electricity. It is toxic.
Substance B: There are two forms of this substance; one is a black, dull, brittle and soft solid. This form conducts electricity. The other form is transparent, very hard and shiny. The melting point of the transparent form is 3730°C.
Substance C: This is a transparent gas with a melting point of −219°C and a boiling point of −183°C. It is essential for respiration in most living things. It does not conduct electricity.
Substance D: This is an unreactive gas with a melting point of −272°C and a boiling point of −269°C. It is very light. It does not conduct electricity.
Substance E: This is a reddish shiny solid. It conducts heat and electricity well. It has a melting point of 1082°C and a boiling point of 2580°C.
Substance F: This is a yellow, brittle solid that does not conduct electricity. The melting point is 119°C and the boiling point is 445°C.

For each substance:

- decide if it is a metal or a non-metal, and give your reasons
- try to identify it
- state a use for it.

The melting points and boiling points will help you. You could use the internet to check your ideas and search for uses.

5 Properties of materials

1. Substance A is a **metal / non-metal**. (Draw a circle around the correct answer.)

   My reason(s) for deciding this is / are: ....

   ....

   I think that substance A is ....

   One use for substance A is ....

2. Substance B is a **metal / non-metal**.

   My reason(s) for deciding this is / are: ....

   ....

   I think that substance B is ....

   One use for substance B is ....

3. Substance C is a **meta / non-metal**.

   My reason(s) for deciding this is / are: ....

   ....

   I think that substance C is ....

   One use for substance C is ....

4. Substance D is a **metal / non-metal**.

   My reason(s) for deciding this is / are: ....

   ....

   I think that substance D is ....

   One use for substance D is ....

5. Substance E is a **metal / non-metal**.

   My reason(s) for deciding this is / are: ....

   ....

   I think that substance E is ....

   One use for substance E is ....

6   Substance F is a **metal / non-metal**.

   My reason(s) for deciding this is / are: ....

   ....

   I think that substance F is ....

   One use for substance F is ....

> 5.3 Metal mixtures

Exercise 5.3 Alloys

In this exercise, you will give examples of alloys, and then explain what they are, and why their properties are different from those of the metals they are made from. You will also do some research on alloys.

Focus

1   What is an alloy? ....

2   Give examples of three different alloys. ....

   ....

Practice

3   Pure iron is not strong enough to be useful. Explain, using particle theory, how adding carbon to iron changes its properties.

   ....

   ....

   ....

   ....

   ....

5 Properties of materials

Challenge

4   Choose an alloy. Do some research and find out about it. You could use the library and/or the internet.

The sorts of things you need to include are:

- name of the alloy
- what metals is it made from
- its properties
- how these properties are different from those of the metals it is made from
- when was it discovered
- what uses it has.

You need to make sure that the information you use is relevant and that the sources you choose are unbiased and scientifically accurate.

....

....

....

....

....

....

....

....

....

....

....

....

....

....

> 5.4 Using properties of materials to separate mixtures

Exercise 5.4 Separating mixtures

In this exercise, you will show your understanding of the different methods used to separate mixtures. You will choose equipment for a practical task and explain how to use it. You will also think about safety when doing practical work.

Focus

Zara has a mixture of sand, salt and water in a beaker. She wants to separate the sand, salt and water.

1   List all the pieces of equipment that Zara will need. Choose from the equipment shown here.

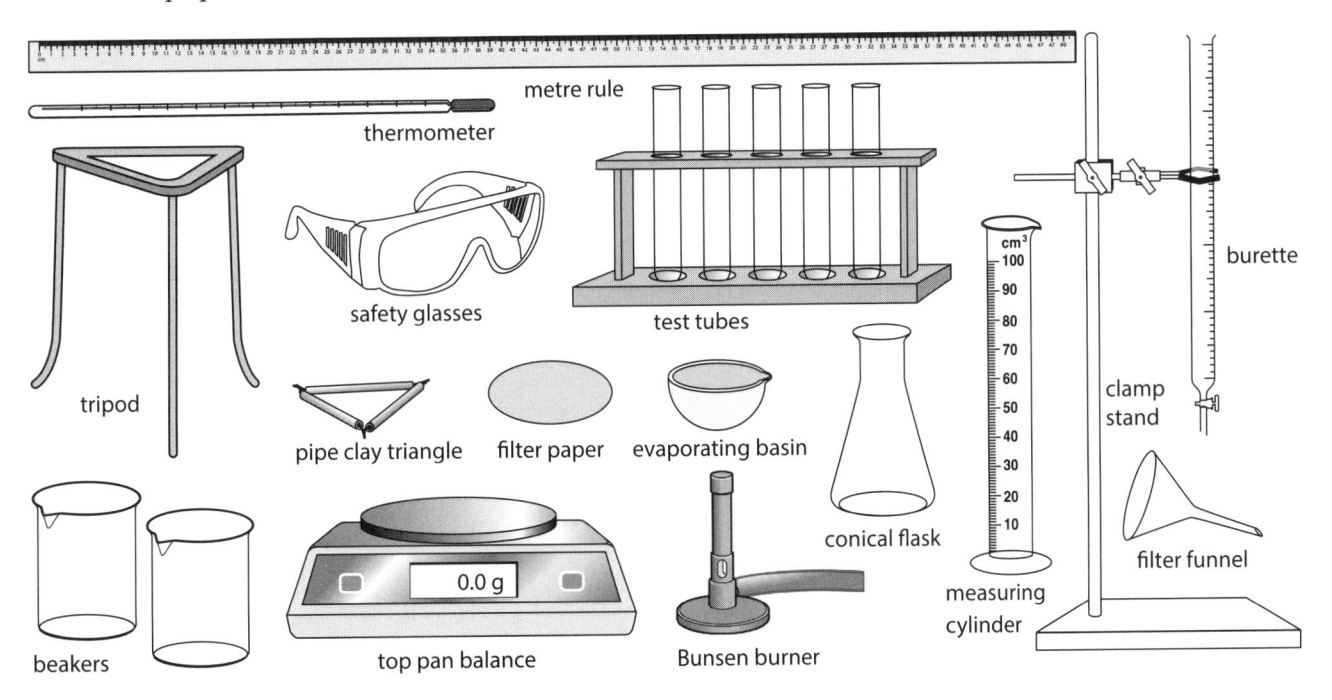

5 Properties of materials

2 Show how to use your chosen equipment to separate out the sand. Draw and label a diagram.

3 Describe anything that Zara needs to be careful about when using this equipment.

....

....

4 Show how to use your chosen equipment to separate out the salt. Draw and label a diagram.

5 State one thing that Zara must do to stay safe when she does this task.

....

....

5.4 Using properties of materials to separate mixtures

Practice

Marcus has dropped a glass bottle of copper sulfate crystals on the floor. He has been given the task of clearing up the mess. He must separate the copper sulfate crystals so they can be used again.

Explain how he does this. For each step, explain why he does that and how he will stay safe.

6   Describe how he will pick the glass and crystals up from the floor.

   ....

   ....

7   Describe how he will separate the glass from the crystals. Which property of the glass and crystals will he use to separate them?

   ....

   ....

   ....

   ....

   ....

   ....

5 Properties of materials

8 Describe how he will make sure he has clean, dry crystals to give back to his teacher.

....

....

....

....

....

....

Challenge

Sofia has a mixture of food dye and water that she wants to separate. At the end, she needs to have clean water and clean food dye. She uses a condenser.

9 Explain how the condenser works to separate the two substances.

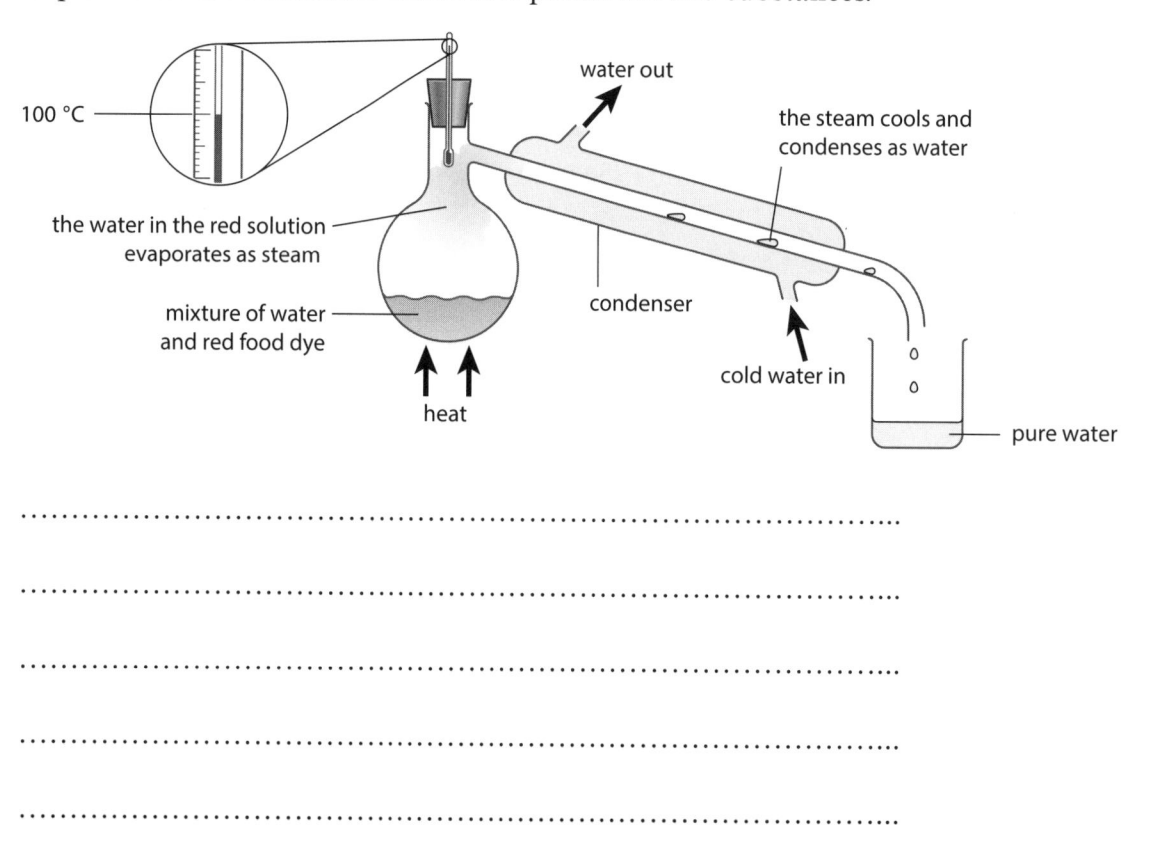

....

....

....

....

....

> 5.5 Acids and alkalis

Exercise 5.5 Acids and alkalis

Focus

1. The words below have a connection with either acids or alkalis. Write each word or group of words in the correct column in the table.

   Remember, some of the words might belong in both columns.

   citric acid   cola   corrosive   lemon juice   harmful
   nitric acid   sharp   sour   sodium hydroxide   soap
   vinegar   washing powder   washing soda

Acid	Alkali

5 Properties of materials

Practice

2 Draw the hazard labels for corrosive and flammable in these boxes.

Corrosive	Flammable

Challenge

3 This table lists some safety points to think about when you use chemicals. Complete the table by explaining the reason for each safety point.

Safety point	Reason
wearing safety glasses	
standing up to work	
placing bottle stoppers upside down on the bench	
replacing the bottle stopper as soon as you have finished using the bottle	
working in an orderly way	

> 5.6 Indicators and the pH scale

Exercise 5.6A Finding mistakes in a table

Focus

In this exercise, you will check facts about acids, alkalis, indicators and the pH scale.

1   Marcus tests some liquids with universal indicator solution.

   Put a cross through each mistake he makes in his results table. Write the correct answer in the space below each crossed-out mistake.

Liquid	Colour with universal indicator solution	pH	Conclusion
lemon juice	yellow	4	weakly alkaline
soap solution	blue/green	8	weakly alkaline
water	green	5	neutral
hydrochloric acid	blue	2	strongly acid
sodium hydroxide	blue/purple	11	strongly alkaline

5 Properties of materials

Exercise 5.6B Indicators

Practice

This exercise will make you think about the practical work that you have done. It is important to be able to describe how you do something.

1   You have used indicators in experiments.
    Explain what an indicator does.

    ....

    ....

2   These diagrams show some laboratory equipment.

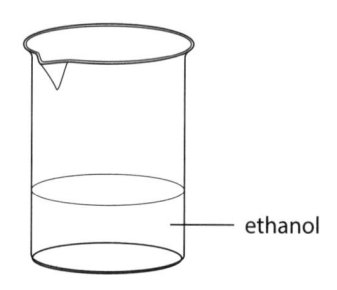

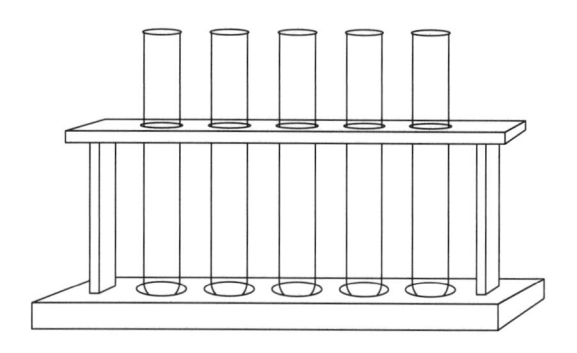

ethanol

106

5.6 Indicators and the pH scale

Describe how you could use the equipment to make your own indicator.

....

....

....

....

....

3 Describe how you would test your indicator to check that it works.

....

....

....

....

4 Explain why an indicator like the one you made cannot help you to find out if coffee or cola is an acid or an alkali.

....

....

....

5 Properties of materials

Exercise 5.6C Indicators

Challenge

In this exercise, you will use information about different indicators to determine the pH.

Zara investigates several indicators. She finds this table in a textbook.

Indicator	pH1	pH4	pH7	pH10	pH13
universal indicator	red	orange	green	blue	purple
phenolphthalein	colourless	colourless	colourless	pink	pink
methyl orange	red	yellow	yellow	yellow	yellow

Zara tests a liquid with some of the indicators. The table shows her results.

Indicator	Colour of the indicator in the test liquid
phenolphthalein	colourless
methyl orange	red

1   Suggest the pH of the liquid.

    ....

2   Explain why universal indicator is more useful than litmus.

    ....

    ....

    ....

6 Earth physics

> ## 6.1 Sound waves

Exercise 6.1 The movement of sound

In this exercise, you will describe the movement in a sound wave.

Focus

1   Zara is playing the violin.

    Sofia hears the sound from the other side of the room.

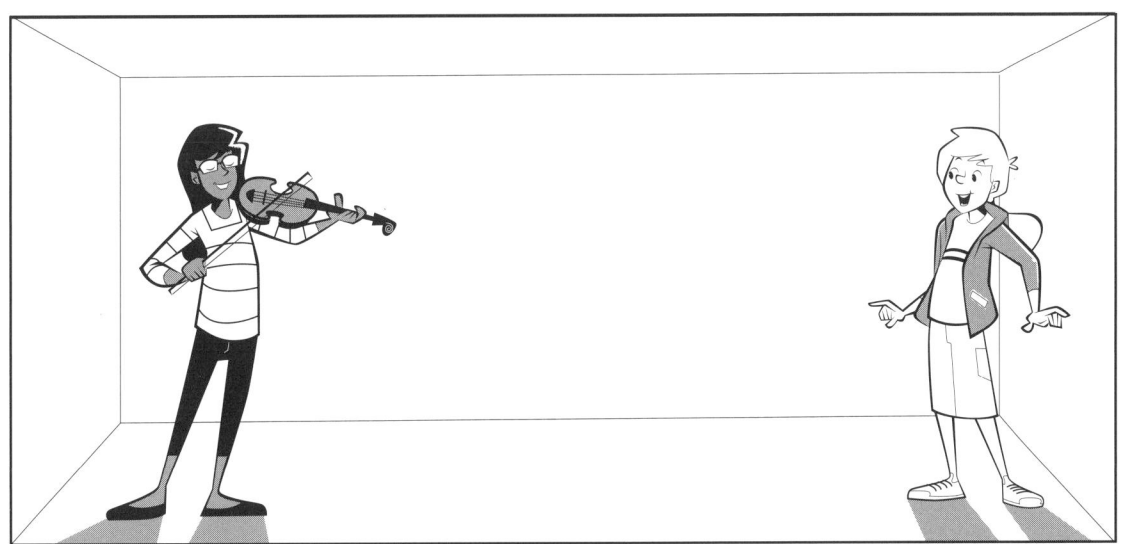

    What must happen for Sofia to hear the sound?

    Tick (✓) one box.

    Objects in the room vibrate. ☐

    Particles in the air vibrate. ☐

    Particles outside the room vibrate. ☐

    The air moves from the violin towards Sofia. ☐

6 Earth physics

2 For each of these statements, write 'true' or 'false'.

Sound travels through solid wood. ....

Sound travels through water. ....

Sound travels through a vacuum. ....

3 Use words from the list to complete the sentence.

vibrate   a vacuum   solids   particles   a gas   liquids

Sound does not travel though .... because

there are no ....

Practice

4 A sound is sent from the bottom of a ship. The sound goes down through the water, as shown in the diagram.

direction of sound wave

What happens in the sound wave?

Tick (✓) one box.

Particles in the water do not move. ☐

Particles in the water vibrate from side to side. ☐

Particles in the water vibrate up and down. ☐

Particles in the water vibrate randomly. ☐

5 Explain why sound does **not** travel in a vacuum.

....

....

....

6.1 Sound waves

6 A loudspeaker is playing loud music.

Sofia holds her hand in front of the loudspeaker cone.

Describe what Sofia will feel when the music is playing.

....

....

....

Challenge

7 A slinky spring is stretched across the floor.

One end of the spring is attached to a clamp.

Marcus holds the other end of the spring.

He makes a wave in the spring that models a sound wave.

    a Draw arrows on the diagram to show how Marcus should move the end of the spring.

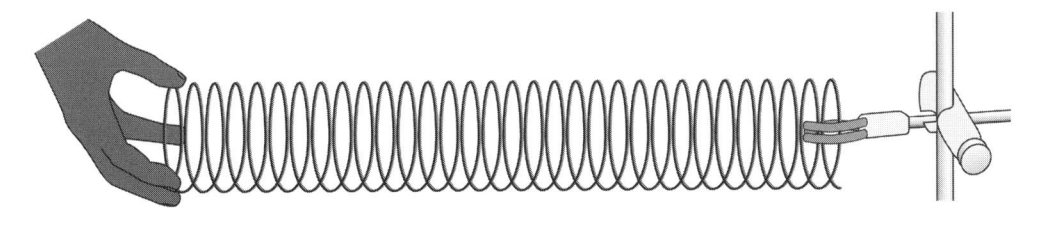

    b In the space below, draw how the spring would appear when modelling a sound wave.

6 Earth physics

8 The speed of a sound wave in air is 340 metres per second.

The speed of a sound wave in solid concrete is 2950 metres per second.

Use ideas about particles to suggest reasons for the difference in speeds.

....

....

....

9 People who work beside aeroplanes wear ear protection.

Explain why loud sounds can damage people's ears.

....

....

....

> 6.2 Reflections of sound

Exercise 6.2 Reflections of sound

In this exercise, you will describe what happens when a sound wave is reflected.

Focus

1 What is the name for a reflected sound wave?

Tick (✓) one box.

sound ☐

vibration ☐

echo ☐

note ☐

6.2 Reflections of sound

2 Which of these will be best at reflecting sound?

Underline the correct answer.

a large tree   tall grass   a flat wall   a sandy beach

3 Arun walks through a tunnel.

When Arun puts his foot down it makes a sound.

Arun then hears the same sound again after a very short time.

Explain why he hears the sound again.

....

....

6 Earth physics

Practice

4 Arun plays the guitar.

One day he plays inside a tunnel, and another day he plays in a field.

Where will Arun hear more echoes? ....
Explain your answer.

....

....

5 Sofia investigates echoes.

She makes the same sound and measures the loudness of the echo from different surfaces.

She uses four different surfaces, A–D.

Her results are shown in the table.

The greater the dB value, the louder the sound.

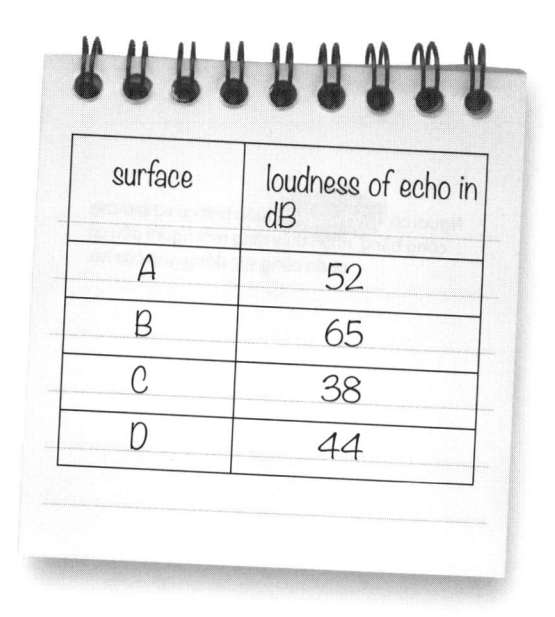

surface	loudness of echo in dB
A	52
B	65
C	38
D	44

a Draw a bar graph of these results on the grid.

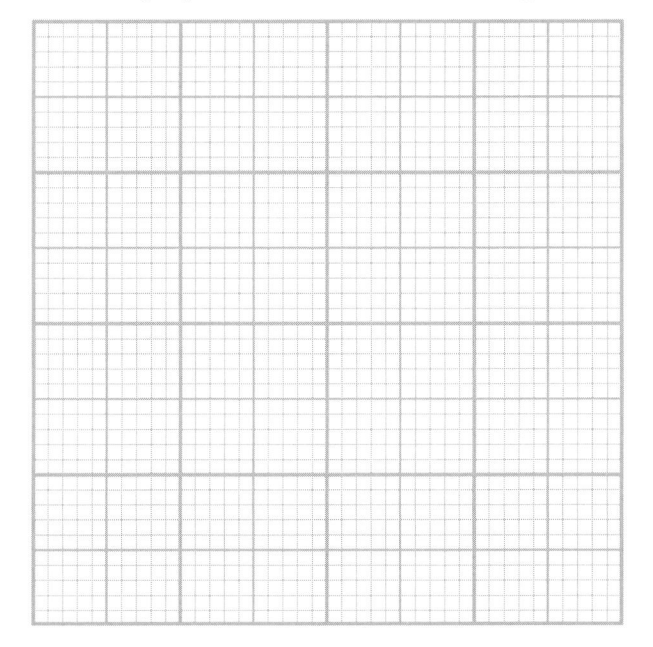

6 Earth physics

b Which surface gives the loudest echo? Write the letter.

....

c Which surface would be best in a room for recording music?

Write the letter. ....

Challenge

6 **Extension question:** The speed of sound in air is 340 metres per second.

Sofia stands 85 metres away from a tall cliff. She bangs a drum loudly.

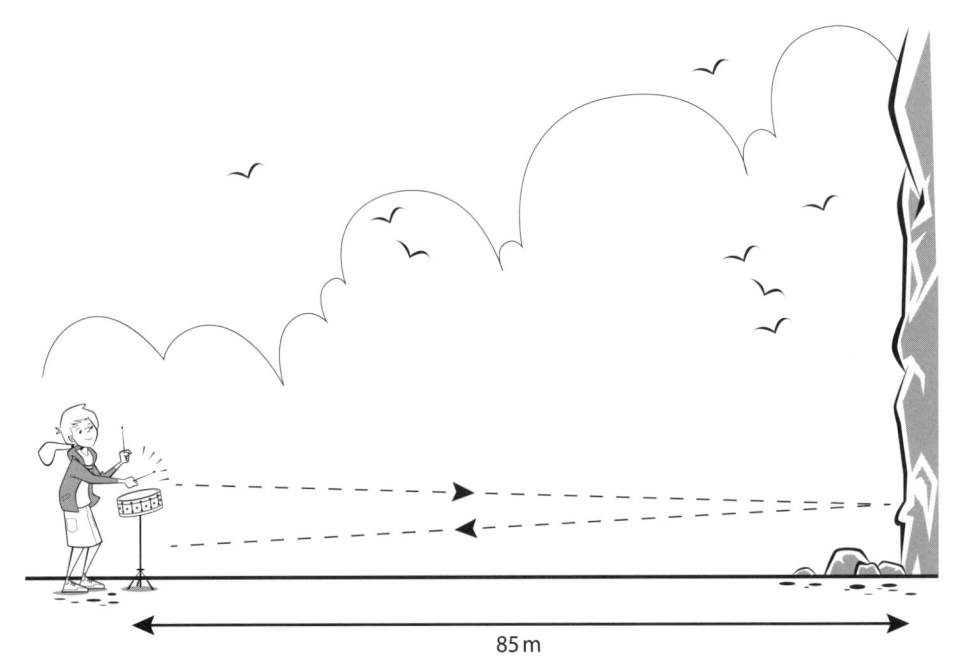

85 m

Calculate the time, in seconds, until she hears the echo of the drum.

Use the equation:

$$\text{Time in seconds} = \frac{\text{distance in metres}}{\text{speed in metres per second}}$$

Show your working.

.... seconds

7 A submarine is a ship that travels under water.

At night or in deep water, people in submarines cannot see what is in front of the submarine.

Explain how a submarine can use echoes of sound to detect objects in the water.

Complete this diagram as part of your answer.

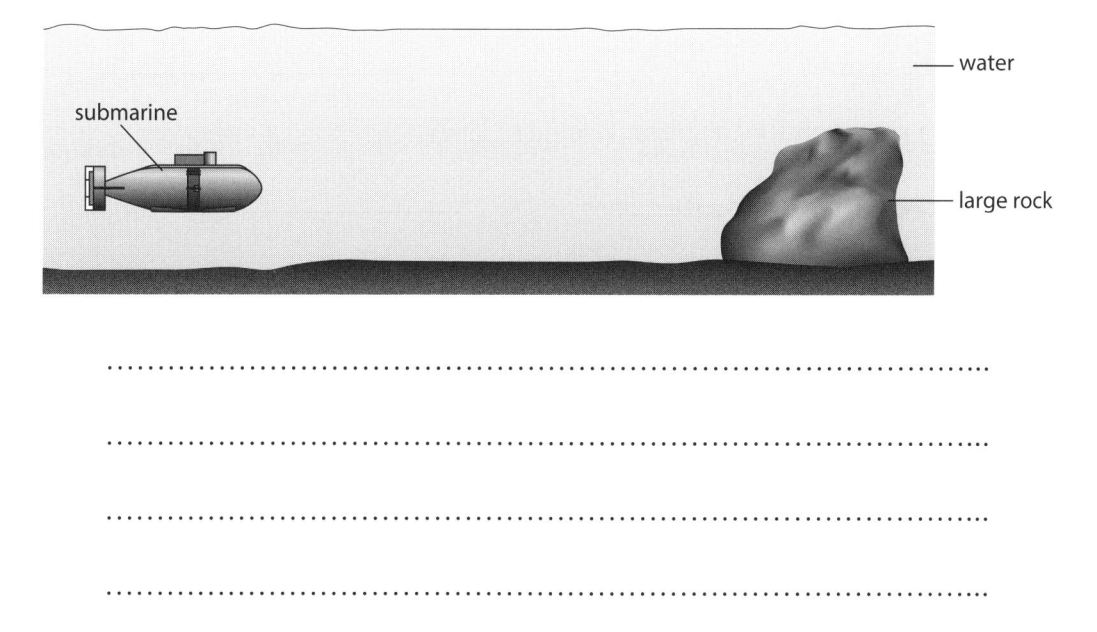

....

....

....

....

6 Earth physics

> 6.3 Structure of the Earth

Exercise 6.3 Continental drift

In this exercise, you will label a diagram of a section through the Earth and look at continental drift.

Focus

1 Label the parts of the Earth shown in the diagram. Use these labels.

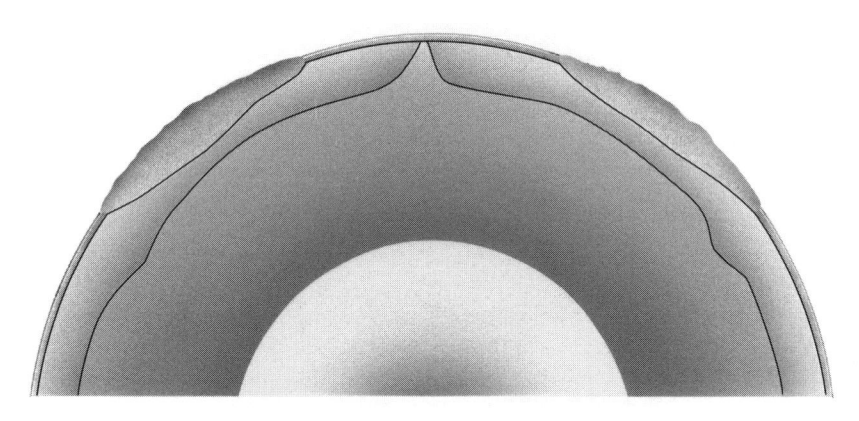

crust   inner core   mantle   outer core

2 Which parts of the Earth are made of:

   a   the metals iron and nickel

   ....

   b   solid rock

   ....

   c   molten (hot liquid) rock and metal

   ....

   d   solid iron and nickel?

   ....

Practice

3 In 1912, Alfred Wegener developed the idea of continental drift. Explain what is meant by 'continental drift'.

....

....

4 Describe the evidence that led Wegener to this idea.

....

....

....

5 Some people did not believe Wegener's idea because he could not explain how continental drift happened. What theory was developed in the 1960s that explained this idea?

....

Challenge

6 How did this theory explain the idea of continental drift?

....

....

....

7 Arun is researching plate tectonics. He finds two websites:

Website 1 states that the tectonic plates move because of flow in the mantle below, causing continental drift.

Website 2 states that the tectonic plates appear to move because the Earth is growing in volume, increasing the distance between all of the continents, then links this with the Earth getting cooler over time.

Briefly evaluate these two information sources for relevance and bias.

....

....

6 Earth physics

> 6.4 Changes in the Earth

Exercise 6.4 How the Earth changes

In this exercise, you will describe how the Earth changes.

Focus

1 What name is given to the line where tectonic plates meet?

   Tick (✓) one box.

   plate boundary ☐

   plate edge ☐

   middle of the plate ☐

   end of the plate ☐

2 What name is given to violent movement between two tectonic plates?

   Underline one word.

   storm   volcano   earthquake   flood

Practice

3 The map shows the South American tectonic plate.

   Mark on the map where:

   a an earthquake would be most likely on land; use the letter E

   b a volcano would be most likely under water; use the letter V

   c fold mountains could be forming on land; use the letter M.

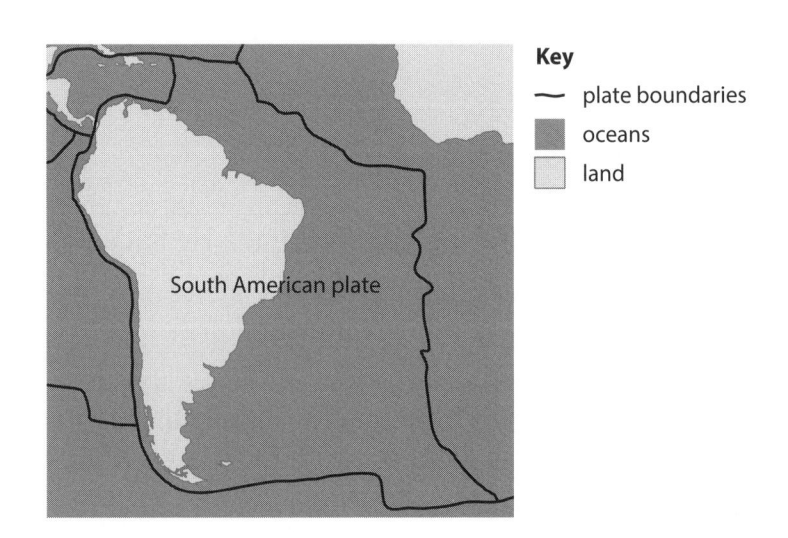

   Key
   — plate boundaries
   ▇ oceans
   ▢ land

Challenge

4 The magnitude of an earthquake is measured on a times 10 scale.

Every time the magnitude number increases by 1, the earthquake becomes 10 times stronger.

For example, a magnitude 5 earthquake is 10 times stronger than magnitude 4.

a How many times stronger is magnitude 6 than magnitude 5?

....

b How many times stronger is magnitude 7 than magnitude 4?

....

5 Earthquakes can happen under the oceans.

a State where these earthquakes are most likely to occur under the oceans.

....

b Earthquakes under the oceans can occur hundreds of kilometres from land.

Explain how these earthquakes can result in damage on land.

....

....

....

6 Earth physics

> 6.5 Solar and lunar eclipses

Exercise 6.5A How eclipses happen

Focus

This exercise will help you think about how eclipses happen.

1 Draw straight lines to match the object to the correct property.

Object	Property
the Moon	gives out its own light
the Sun	does not give out its own light
the Earth	

2 What is formed when an opaque object blocks rays of light?

Tick (✓) one box.

- reflection ☐
- shadow ☐
- light ☐
- sound ☐

3 Use the words from the list to complete the sentences.

the Sun   the Moon   the Earth

a A solar eclipse happens when .... comes between .... and ....

b A lunar eclipse happens when .... comes between .... and ....

6.5 Solar and lunar eclipses

Exercise 6.5B Diagrams of eclipses

Practice

In this exercise you will draw diagrams to show how eclipses happen.

1   Complete these diagrams to show how eclipses happen.

   You will need to draw:
   - the Earth in the correct position
   - the Moon in the correct position
   - rays of light coming from the Sun in both diagrams.

   Use a ruler for drawing the rays of light.

   Add labels to your diagram.

   Try to draw the diagrams without copying from somewhere else.

   a   Solar eclipse

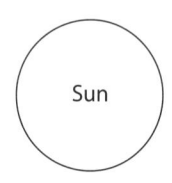

   b   Lunar eclipse

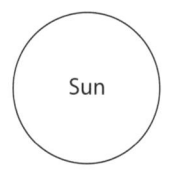

6 Earth physics

Exercise 6.5C More detail on eclipses

Challenge

In this exercise you will think in detail about eclipses and how they happen.

1. Draw a diagram to show how a solar eclipse happens.

   Include:
   - the Sun
   - the Moon
   - the Earth
   - rays of light from the Sun
   - a label to show where there is a total eclipse
   - a label to show where there is a partial eclipse.

   Try to draw the diagram yourself, without copying from somewhere else.

2. Arun hears two people talking.

   One person says: 'I saw a lunar eclipse in the middle of the day.'

   Draw a labelled diagram to show why this statement cannot be true.

7 Microorganisms in the environment

> 7.1 Microorganisms

Exercise 7.1 Microorganisms experiment

In this exercise, you will practise following instructions. You will also think about variables in an experiment.

Focus

1   Marcus does an experiment to compare the number of microorganisms in the air in Classroom 203 and Classroom 204.

   These are the instructions that the teacher gives Marcus for Classroom 203.

   > ① Collect a dish containing sterile agar jelly.
   > ② Label the base of the dish with the number of the classroom you are testing.
   > ③ Place the dish in the classroom and take off the lid.
   > ④ After five minutes, put the lid back on.
   > ⑤ Use a small strip of tape to stick the lid onto the base.
   > ⑥ Place the dish, upside down, in a safe place in the laboratory.

   The pictures show Marcus following the instructions. They are not in the correct order.

7 Microorganisms in the environment

Write a number in the box next to each picture to show which instruction Marcus is carrying out.

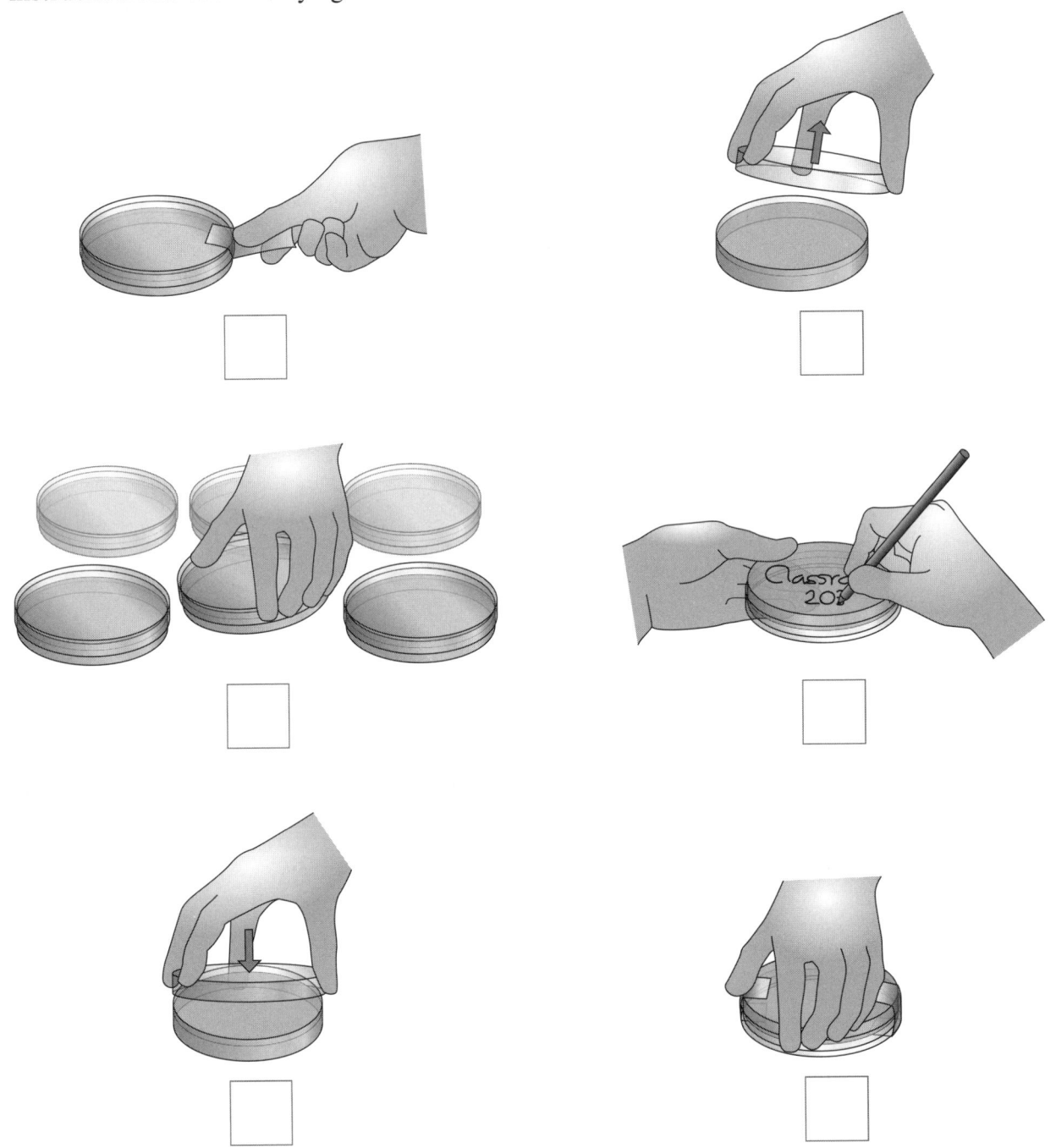

☐

☐

☐

☐

☐

☐

7.1 Microorganisms

Practice

2 Marcus needs to complete his experiment. He follows the instructions again, but this time he puts the dish into Classroom 204.

A **variable** is something that can change in an experiment.

Usually, you change one variable and keep other variables the same.

Which variables should Marcus keep the same?

You only need to think about variables that might affect Marcus's results.

Tick (✓) all the correct ones.

the room where he puts the dish ☐

the type of jelly in the dish ☐

the length of time he leaves the lid off ☐

the type of pen he uses to label the dish ☐

3 The diagram shows the two dishes after they have been left in the laboratory for five days.

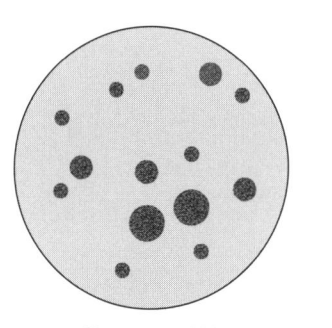

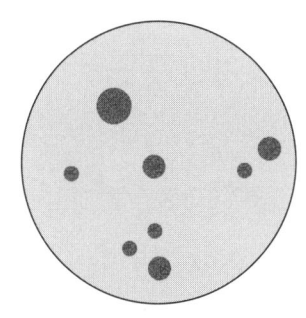

Classroom 203   Classroom 204

Complete this conclusion that Marcus can make from his experiment:

There are .... microorganisms in the air in Classroom 203 than in Classroom 204.

127

7 Microorganisms in the environment

Challenge

4   Marcus decides to do another experiment with Petri dishes and agar jelly. His teacher asks him to write an hypothesis that he can test.

Which hypothesis could Marcus test? Tick (✓) **one** answer.

All bacteria are single-celled. ☐

Bacteria grow faster at a temperature of 30 °C than at 10 °C. ☐

Bacterial cells are smaller than yeast cells. ☐

5   Describe how Marcus can do an experiment to test the hypothesis you have chosen.

....

....

....

....

....

....

....

....

....

> 7.2 Food chains and webs

Exercise 7.2A Arctic hares

Focus

In this task, you will use information to change four food chains into one food web.

Arctic hare

Arctic wolf

Here are four food chains involving Arctic hares.

Arctic willow ⟶ Arctic hare ⟶ snowy owl ⟶ Arctic wolf

purple saxifrage ⟶ Arctic hare ⟶ Arctic fox ⟶ Arctic wolf

grasses ⟶ Arctic hare ⟶ gyrfalcon

Arctic willow ⟶ Arctic hare ⟶ Arctic wolf

Construct a food web from the four food chains.

7 Microorganisms in the environment

Exercise 7.2B Building up a food web

Practice

In this exercise, you will practise drawing a food web. You will also practise using the correct terms to describe the different organisms in a food web.

The diagram shows a food chain in a sea grass forest in the sea in Central America.

```
        humans
          ↑
          |
          |
       queen conch
          ↑
          |
          |
        sea grass
```

The arrows in the food chain show how energy flows from one organism to the next. This happens when one organism eats another.

1   Sea urchins eat sea grass.

    Add sea urchins to the diagram.

Make sure you draw an arrow going to the sea urchins from their food.

2   Pen shells also eat sea grass. Add pen shells to the diagram.

3   Phytoplankton are tiny, microscopic protoctists. They are eaten by sea urchins, queen conch and pen shells.

    Add phytoplankton to the diagram.

4 Helmet snails and stingrays both eat sea urchins and pen shells.

Add helmet snails and stingrays to the diagram.

5 Humans eat helmet snails and stingrays.

Add arrows to the diagram to show this.

6 Which organisms are the producers in your food web?

....

....

7 Name **two** herbivores in the food web.

....

....

8 Name **two** carnivores in the food web.

....

....

7 Microorganisms in the environment

Exercise 7.2C Constructing a food web

Challenge

In this exercise, you will use information to construct a food web. It is a good idea to identify the producers first and put them at the bottom of the web. Then build up carefully from there. Remember to make all the arrows point in the correct direction.

Here is information about some of the organisms that live on grassy plains in Africa.

- Giraffes and impala (a kind of antelope) eat the leaves from acacia trees.
- Locusts and grass rats eat grass.
- Wild dogs, cheetahs and lions are predators of all of the vertebrate herbivores.
- Many kinds of birds eat locusts.
- Eagles eat birds.

1 In the space below, construct a food web for this habitat.

2 Draw a green circle around each producer in your food web.

3 Draw a blue circle around each herbivore in your food web.

4 Draw a red circle around each carnivore in your food web.

> 7.3 Microorganisms and decay

Exercise 7.3A Decomposers in a compost heap

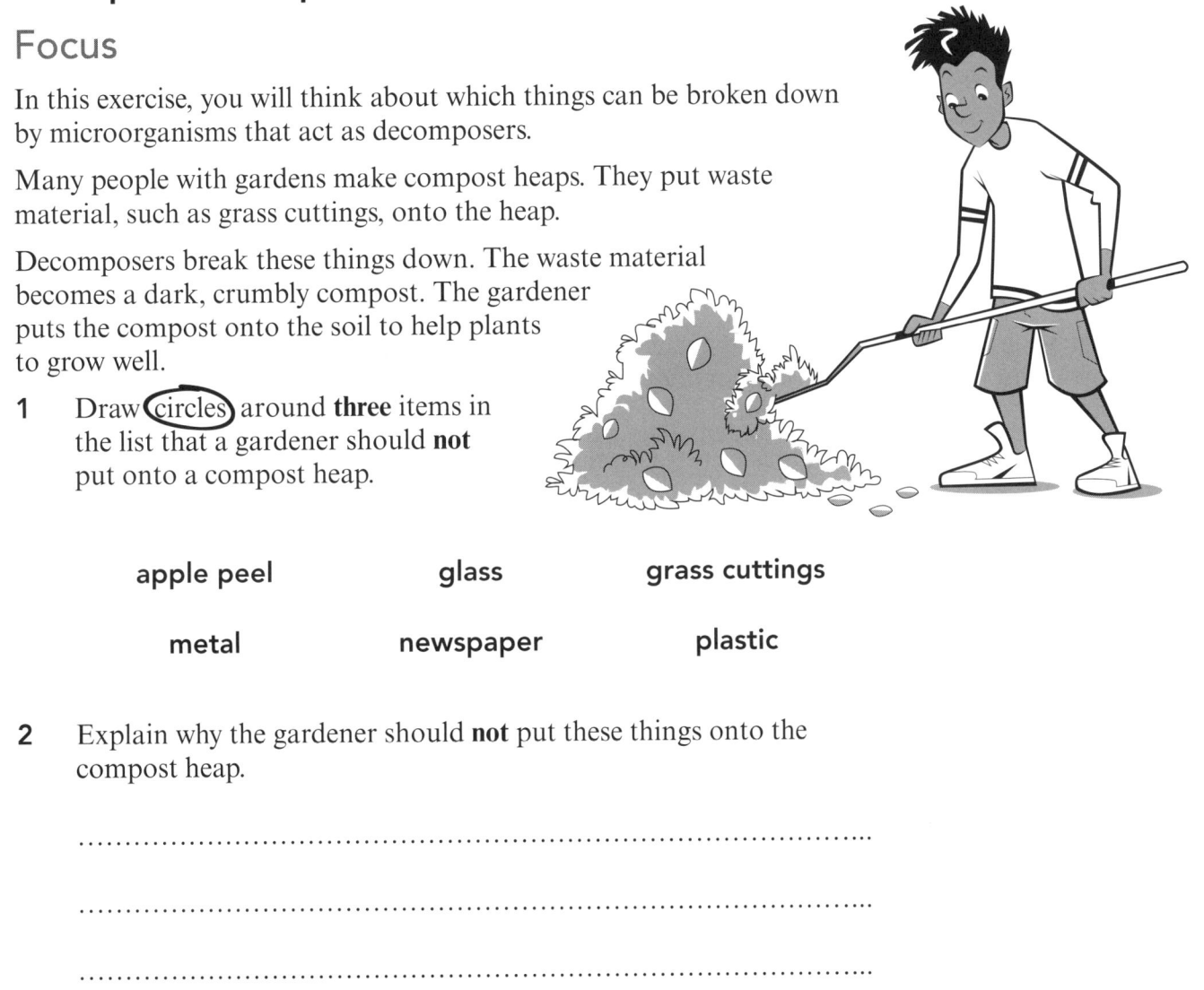

Focus

In this exercise, you will think about which things can be broken down by microorganisms that act as decomposers.

Many people with gardens make compost heaps. They put waste material, such as grass cuttings, onto the heap.

Decomposers break these things down. The waste material becomes a dark, crumbly compost. The gardener puts the compost onto the soil to help plants to grow well.

1   Draw circles around **three** items in the list that a gardener should **not** put onto a compost heap.

   apple peel   glass   grass cuttings

   metal   newspaper   plastic

2   Explain why the gardener should **not** put these things onto the compost heap.

   ....

   ....

   ....

7 Microorganisms in the environment

3 Imagine that you have some material from a compost heap in your school laboratory.

Explain how you could find out if there are microorganisms in it.

....

....

....

....

Exercise 7.3B Investigating leaf decay

Practice

This exercise gives you practice in thinking about how to do an experiment to test an idea. You will also think about presenting results and using evidence to make conclusions.

Arun knows that some microorganisms are decomposers. They cause dead leaves to decay.

He predicts that bigger organisms, such as earthworms and other tiny animals in the soil, might also help to make leaves decay.

In June, Arun makes two identical small bags out of nets with different-sized mesh.

Bag A 1 cm mesh

Earthworms and other small animals can get through the holes.

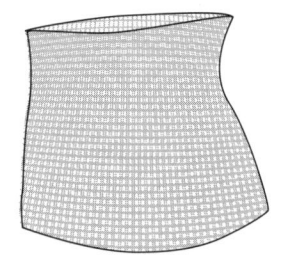

Bag B 0.005 mm mesh

Only microorganisms can get through the holes.

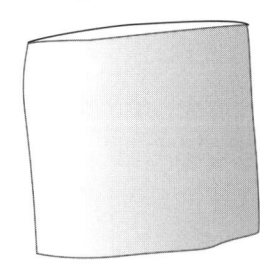

Next, Arun collects some dead leaves. He carefully cuts rectangles measuring 1 cm × 2 cm from the leaves. He puts 50 leaf rectangles into each bag.

He buries the bags close to each other in the soil in his garden.

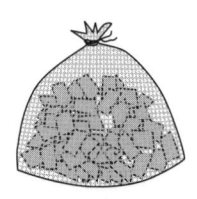

Every two months, he digs up the bags and measures how much of the leaves has disappeared from each bag.

The graph shows Arun's results.

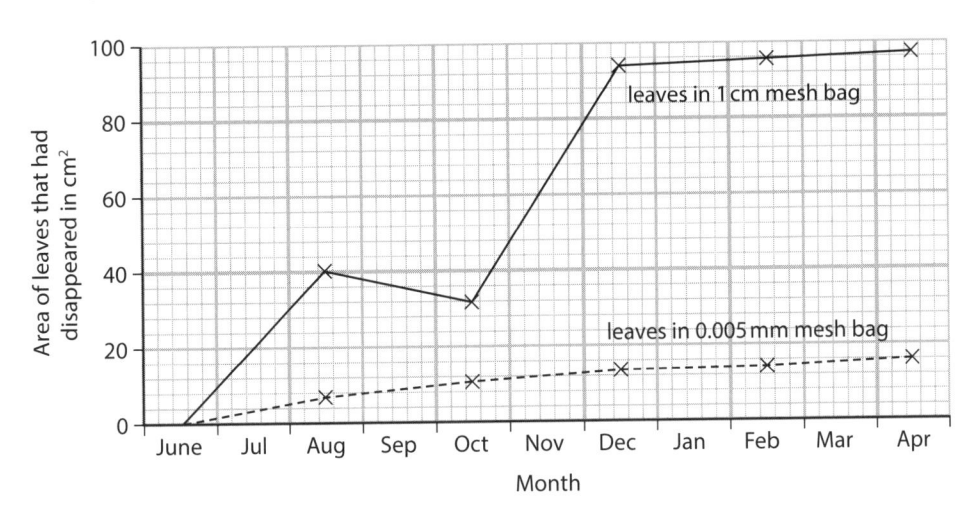

1. Arun decides that one of his results is wrong. He must have made a mistake when he was making his measurements.

   Which result is wrong?

   ....

2. In which bag did the largest area of leaves disappear during Arun's experiment?

   ....

3. Which organisms could reach the leaves in this bag?

   ....

4. Arun decides that his prediction was correct.
   Explain the evidence that he has for this decision.

   ....

   ....

   ....

   ....

   ....

Exercise 7.3C Analysing data about mould on bread

Challenge

In this challenging task, you will use results from an experiment to construct a line graph, analyse the results and make a conclusion. You will also use information to suggest an explanation.

Sofia and Zara investigate how temperature affects the growth of mould on moist bread.

They take some slices of bread and cut them into 15 equal-sized pieces.

They place three pieces in each of five identical dishes. The diagram shows one of the dishes.

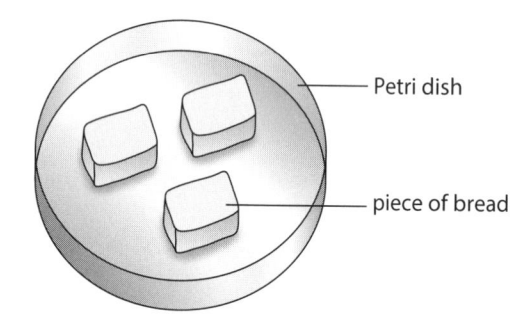

The girls add the same volume of water to each dish – just enough to make sure the bread is damp.

They then place the dishes in five containers, each kept at a different temperature, ranging from $-4\,°C$ to $60\,°C$.

They leave the dishes in the containers for three days. Each day, they add a small volume of water to each dish to keep the bread damp.

7.3 Microorganisms and decay

On the fourth day, the girls measure the area of the bread that has mould growing on it. Their results are shown in the table.

Dish	Temperature in °C	Area of mould growth in mm²			
		Bread sample 1	Bread sample 2	Bread sample 3	Mean
1	−4	0	1	0	0.3
2	10	2	3	3	2.7
3	20	12	8	9	9.7
4	40	14	5	18	
5	60	10	12	13	

1. Suggest how the girls could estimate the area of mould growing on the bread.

   ....

   ....

   ....

2. One of the results for the dish kept at 40 °C does not fit the pattern of all the other results. It is an **anomalous** result. Draw a (circle) around the anomalous result.

3. Ignoring the result you have circled, calculate the mean area of mould growth for the dishes kept at 40 °C.

   To do this, add the other two results and divide by 2.

   Write your answer in the table.

4. Calculate the mean area of mould growth in the dish kept at 60 °C. Write your answer to one decimal place.

   Remember that when you write numbers to one decimal place:

   32.48 becomes 32.5

   32 becomes 32.0

   Write your answer in the table.

7 Microorganisms in the environment

5 Construct a line graph on the grid, showing the mean area of mould growth at different temperatures.

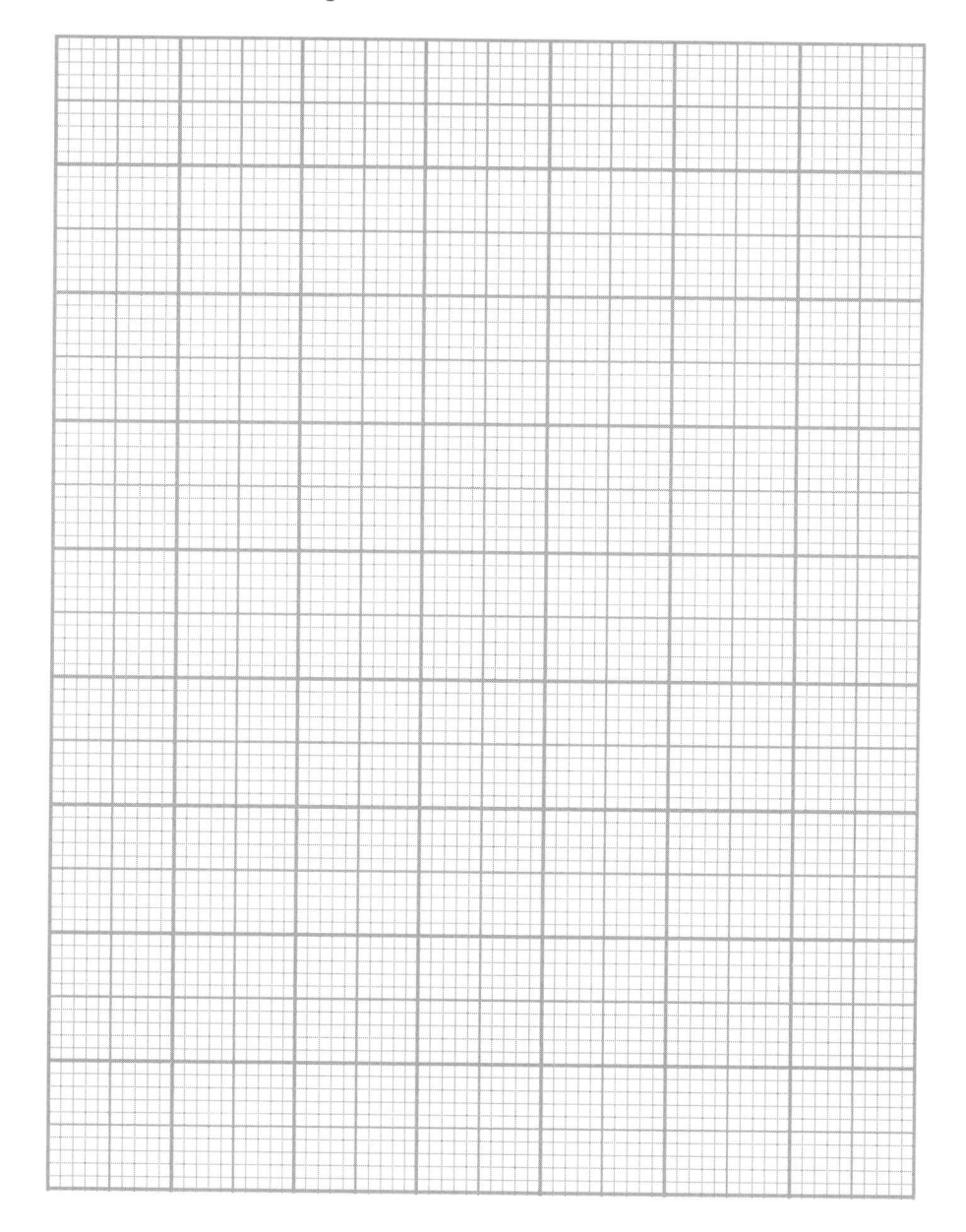

6 Suggest why the results for the three bread samples at a particular temperature are not exactly the same.

....

....

7.3 Microorganisms and decay

7 Use the girls' results to make a conclusion.

....

....

....

8 Sofia found some information on the internet:

> All cells, including microorganisms, are kept alive by chemical reactions that happen inside the cells. The faster the reactions happen, the faster the microorganism grows and reproduces.
>
> Chemical reactions happen faster when it is warm than when it is cold. The reactions take place very slowly, or not at all, at low temperatures, but speed up at higher temperatures. However, at very high temperatures, the reactions stop.

Use the information that Sofia found to suggest an explanation for the girls' results. Write your answer in your own words.

....

....

....

....

....

....

....

....

7 Microorganisms in the environment

> 7.4 Microorganisms in food webs

Exercise 7.4 Microorganisms in food webs

Focus

1   Write the correct word or words next to each description. Choose words from the list. You can use each word once, more than once or not at all.

bacterium   decomposer   food web   microorganism   producer

a   An organism that is so small it cannot be seen without a microscope.

    ....

b   A diagram showing how energy passes from one organism to another.

    ....

c   An organism that feeds by decaying organic matter.

    ....

Practice

2   In a meadow, grasshoppers and caterpillars eat grass. Lizards eat grasshoppers. Small birds eat caterpillars. Hawks eat lizards and small birds.

Use this information to construct a food web. Include decomposers in your food web.

7.4 Microorganisms in food webs

Challenge

3   Biologists who study ecology know that microorganisms have an important role to play in the environment.

Describe the ecological role that some microorganisms have as decomposers.

....

....

....

....

....

....

....

....

8 Changes to materials

> 8.1 Simple chemical reactions

Exercise 8.1A Physical and chemical reactions

Focus

In this exercise you will identify physical and chemical changes.

1   Tick (✓) all the correct statements.

In a physical change, no new substances are formed.	☐
When iron atoms bond with sulfur atoms, it is a chemical change.	☐
When ice melts to form water, it is a chemical change.	☐
When your cells use food to release energy, it is a physical change.	☐
When you cook an egg, it is a chemical change.	☐
When you let off fireworks, it is a physical change.	☐

8.1 Simple chemical reactions

2   In the chemical change shown here, oxygen reacts with hydrogen to form water.

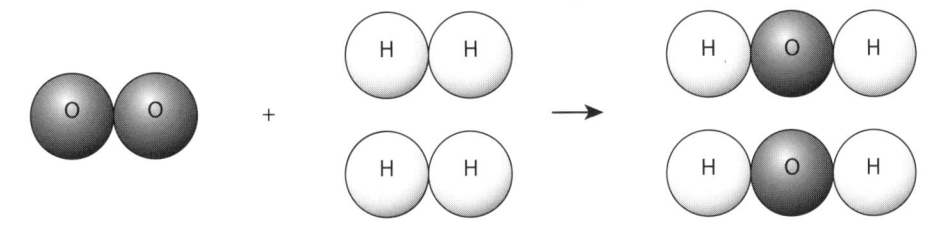

    a   The compound that is made in this reaction is

        ………………………………… .

    b   The elements that make this compound are

        ………………………………… .

    c   The reactants in this reaction are ……………………………… .

Exercise 8.1B Atoms in chemical reactions

Practice

In this exercise you will develop your understanding of how atoms are rearranged in a chemical reaction.

1   When magnesium is burnt in air, one atom of magnesium bonds with one atom of oxygen.

    a   In the circles of this particle diagram, write the symbols of the elements that make up the product.

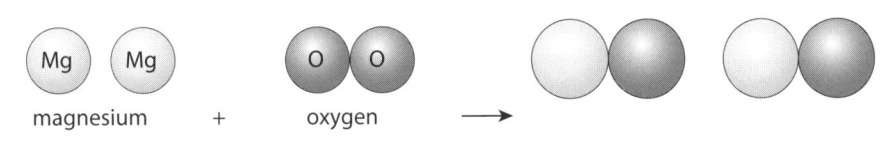

        magnesium + oxygen →

        …………………………………

    b   Write the name of the product in the space below the diagram.

2   When an acid is added to a metal it bubbles and gives off a gas. What is the name of the gas?

    ………………………………………………………………………

8 Changes to materials

3 How would you test for this gas?

....

....

4 Complete these word equations.

    a   zinc + ... acid ⟶ zinc chloride + ...

    b   .... + sulfuric acid ⟶ magnesium sulfate + ...

5 The products of a chemical reaction contain the elements magnesium, hydrogen and chlorine. What elements are present in the reactants?

....

....

Exercise 8.1C Metal and acid

Challenge

In this exercise you will plot a graph of some data for a metal–acid reaction, and interpret the results.

Arun and Marcus reacted a metal with an acid. They used the apparatus shown in the diagram to measure the volume of gas given off when acid was added to the metal. They measured the volume of the gas **only** when all the metal had disappeared.

The boys investigated how changing the mass of metal used would change the volume of gas produced.

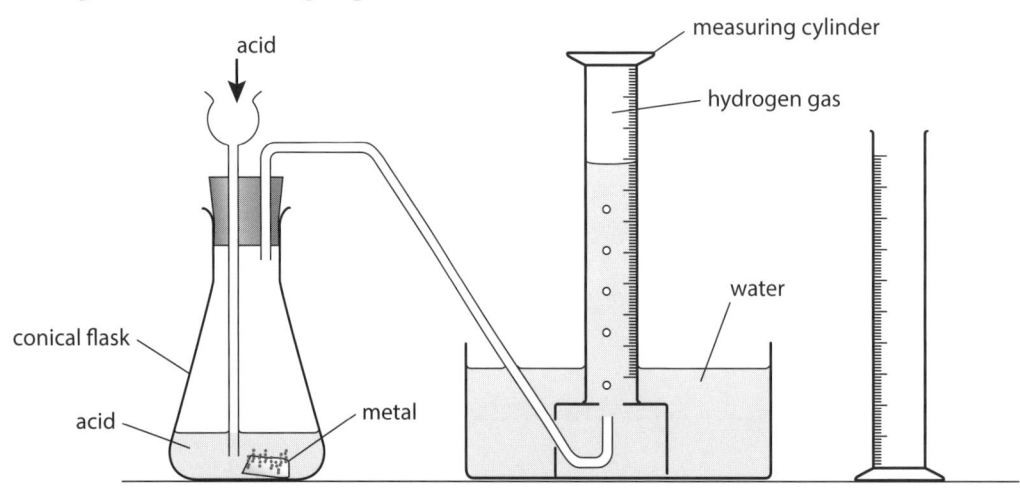

These are the results.

Mass of metal that reacted in g	Volume of hydrogen given off in cm^3
0.5	70
1.0	120
1.5	150
2.0	220
2.5	260
3.0	310
3.5	350
4.0	410
4.5	450
5.0	510

8 Changes to materials

1. Plot the data in a graph on the grid, and draw a line of best fit.

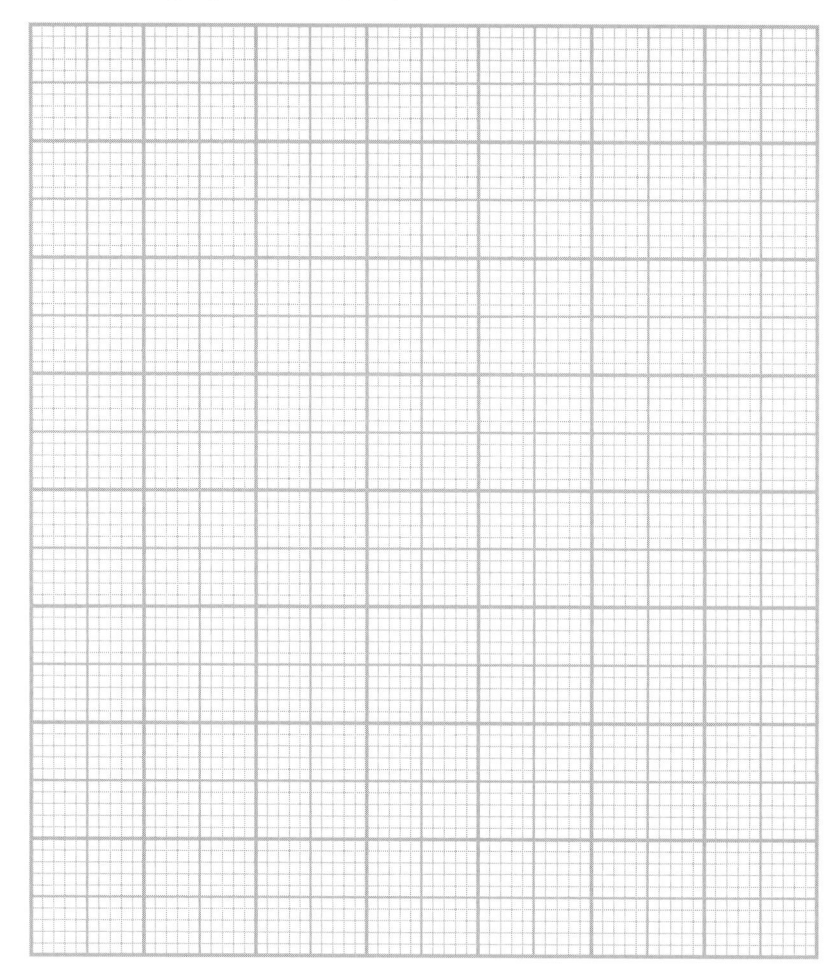

2. What conclusions can you make from the results?

   ....

   ....

3. If you did this experiment but only had measuring cylinders that held 100 cm³, what problem would you have in getting accurate results?

   ....

   ....

4 The reactants used in this investigation were zinc and sulfuric acid. What were the products?

....

5 If magnesium and hydrochloric acid had been used, what would the products have been?

....

> 8.2 Neutralisation

Exercise 8.2A Measuring

Focus

In this exercise you will practise reading measurements from measuring cylinders and burettes.

1 The diagrams, A–E, show measuring cylinders with liquid in them. Write the volume of liquid in each measuring cylinder. One has been done for you as an example.

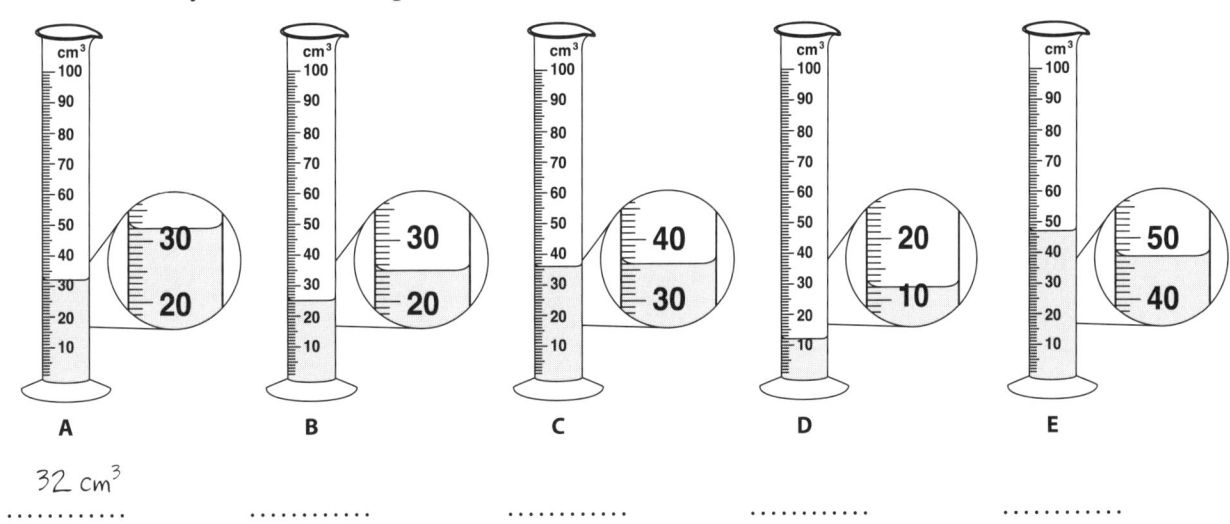

A: 32 cm³

B: .... C: .... D: .... E: ....

- Remember that the surface of the liquid is slightly curved. This curved surface is called the meniscus.
- The volume of the liquid is measured from the bottom of the curve.
- Do not forget to include the units with your answers.

8 Changes to materials

2 The diagrams A–E show burettes with no liquid in them.
Mark the level of the liquid at these volumes.
One has been done for you as an example.

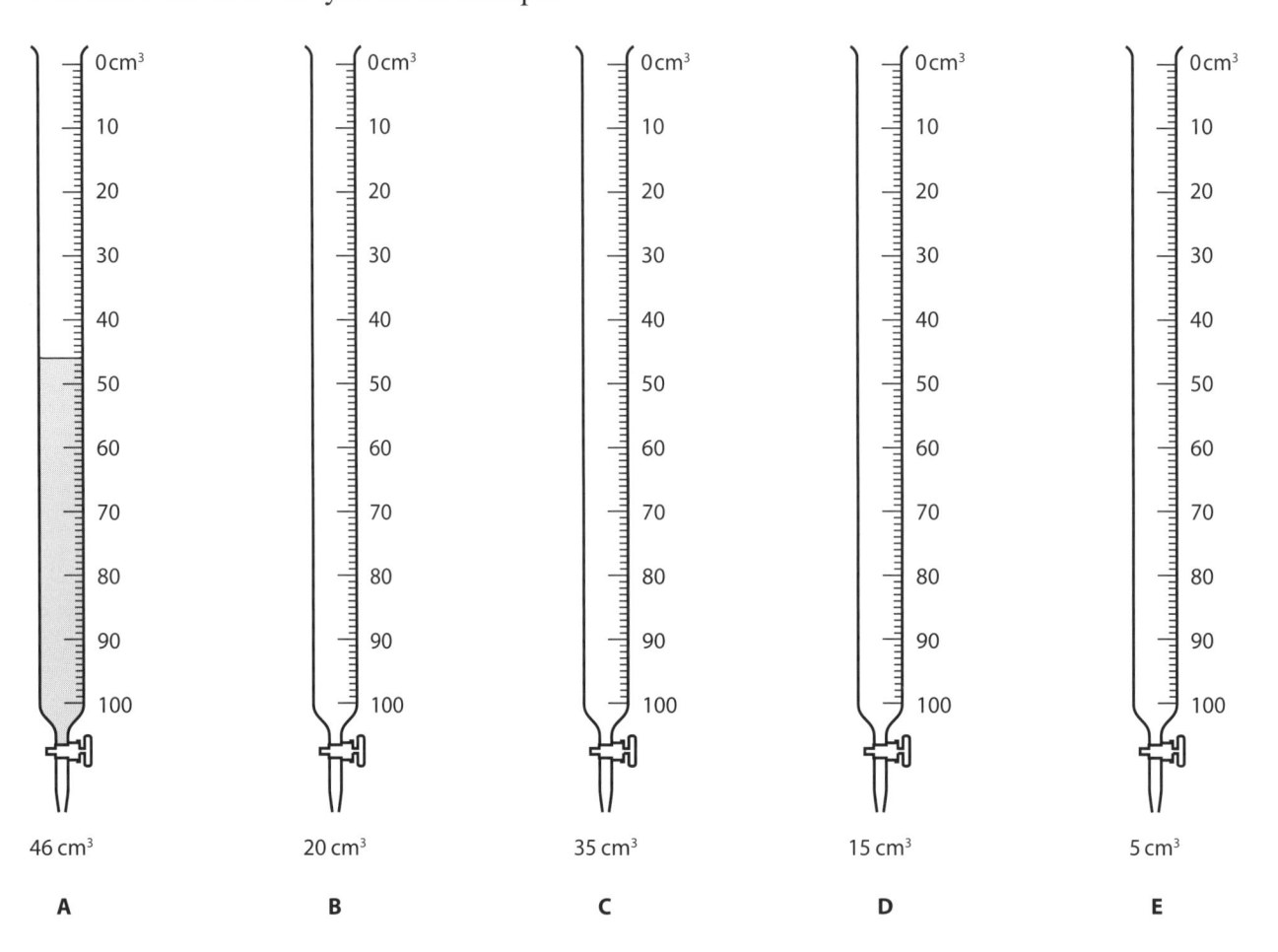

46 cm³	20 cm³	35 cm³	15 cm³	5 cm³
A	B	C	D	E

- Remember that the surface of the liquid (meniscus) is slightly curved.
- The volume of liquid is measured from the bottom of the curve.
- The scale on the burette starts with zero at the top.

Practice

3 The diagram shows some burettes with different volumes of liquid in them. Write down the reading on each burette. Remember to include the units.

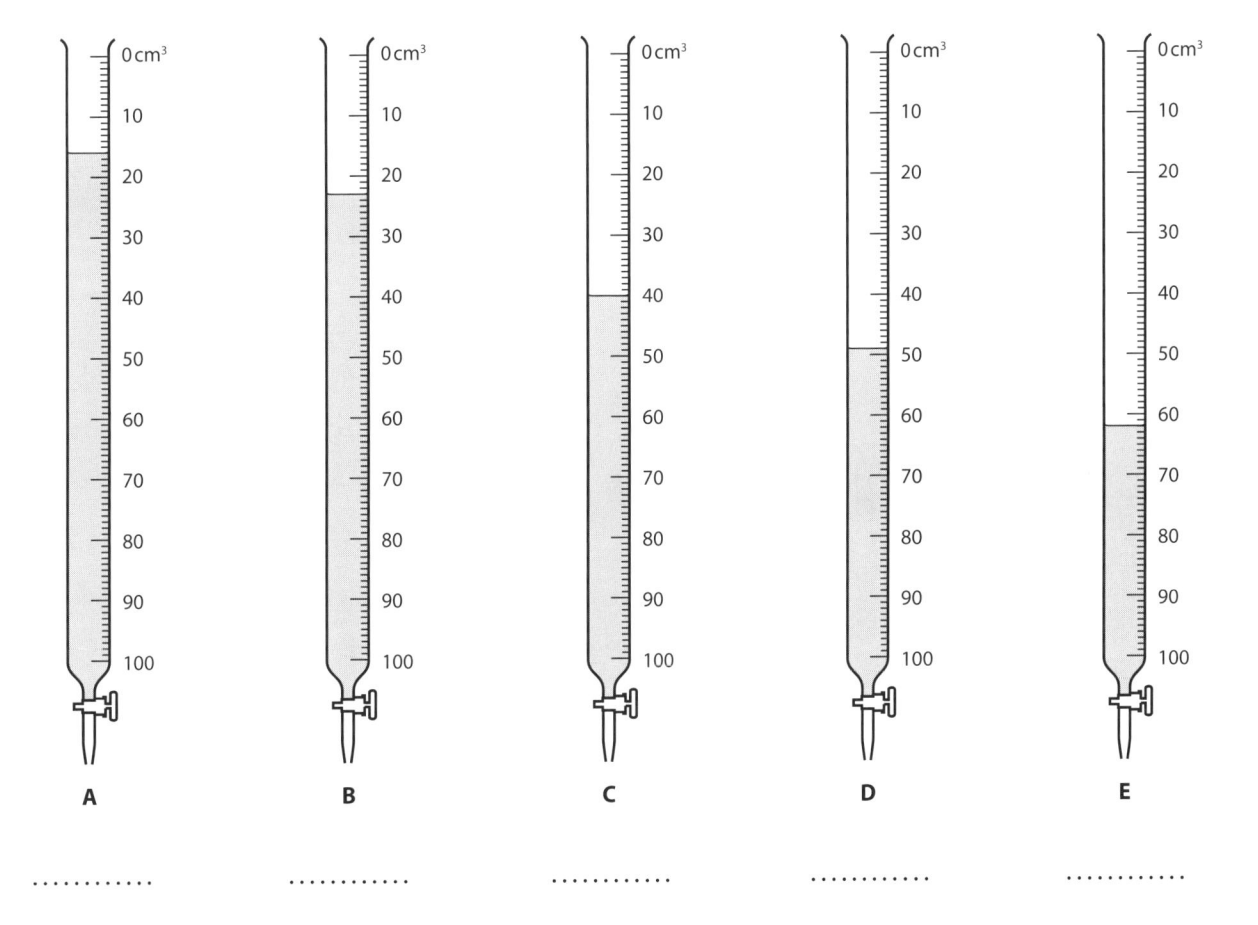

A ....

B ....

C ....

D ....

E ....

8 Changes to materials

Exercise 8.2B Neutralising a

Challenge

In this task you will identify some unsafe behaviour and mistakes made in a student's practical work with acids and alkalis. Then you will suggest ways to correct these mistakes.

This is some homework handed in by a student after some class practical work on neutralisation.

They were given these pieces of apparatus and chemicals.

This report shows that the student did not work safe

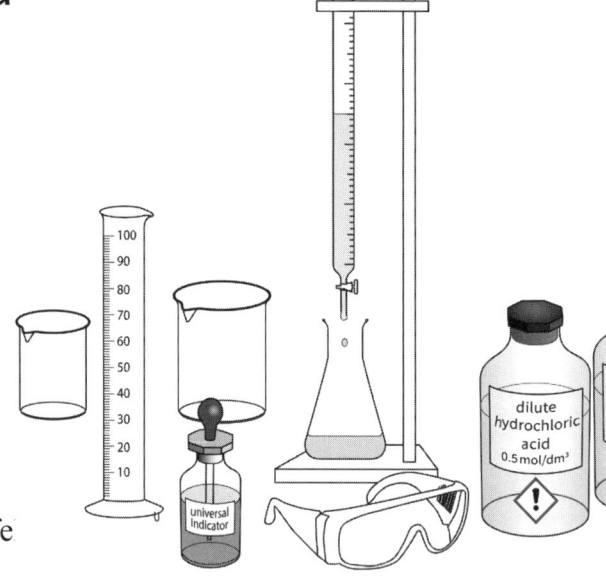

My practical work on neutralisation

I got on with my work quickly and went to get the chemicals.

I didn't wear the goggles because they hurt my nose.

Everyone was queuing to get the acid from the teacher.

This was marked 0.5 mol/dm³.

I didn't want to wait and there was another acid on the shelf behind the teacher's desk, so I used that – hydrochloric acid 1.0 mol/dm³.

I took the bottle to my desk and poured some in a beaker. It was about half full. I poured in about half a bottle of universal indicator.

It went red.

I used the sodium hydroxide that the teacher put on the desk.

I added it straight into the beaker. I stirred it to see if it would go green, but it went blue at once.

So I added more acid and it went red. I tipped it all into a bigger beaker becasue there was too much liquid.

It was taking much too long, so I guessed how much alkali to use.

Write the correct method for neutralising acid, to show the student how the practical work should have been done.

You need to explain how to work safely at each step and use the correct names for equipment.

8.3 Investigating acids and alkalis

Exercise 8.3A Indigestion investigation

Focus

In this exercise you will make sure an investigation is a fair test.

When your stomach makes too much acid, you have indigestion. You can take medicine to help this. The medicine is an alkali and it neutralises the acid.

Marcus tests some indigestion medicines to see how well they work. He finds out how much of each medicine is needed to neutralise some acid. He has three types of powdered medicine to test.

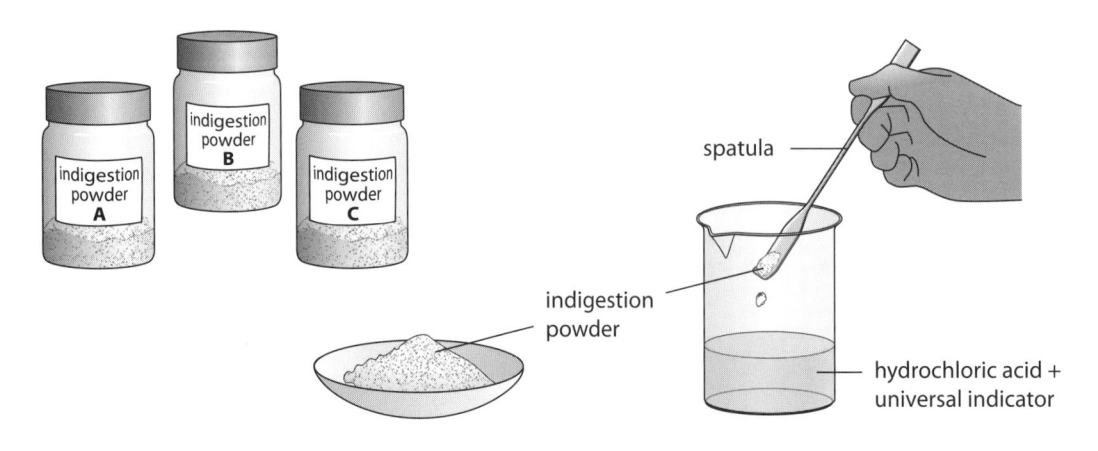

8.3 Investigating acids and alkalis

He watches for the acid plus universal indicator to turn green.
He counts the number of spatulas of each powder he needs to do this.

This is his table to record the results.

1   Write a heading for the second column.

Powder	
A	
B	
C	

2   Other students in Marcus's class do some tests.

Look at the diagrams of what they do. Decide if each is a fair test or not.

Under each set of diagrams write **fair** or **not fair**.

Arun's test

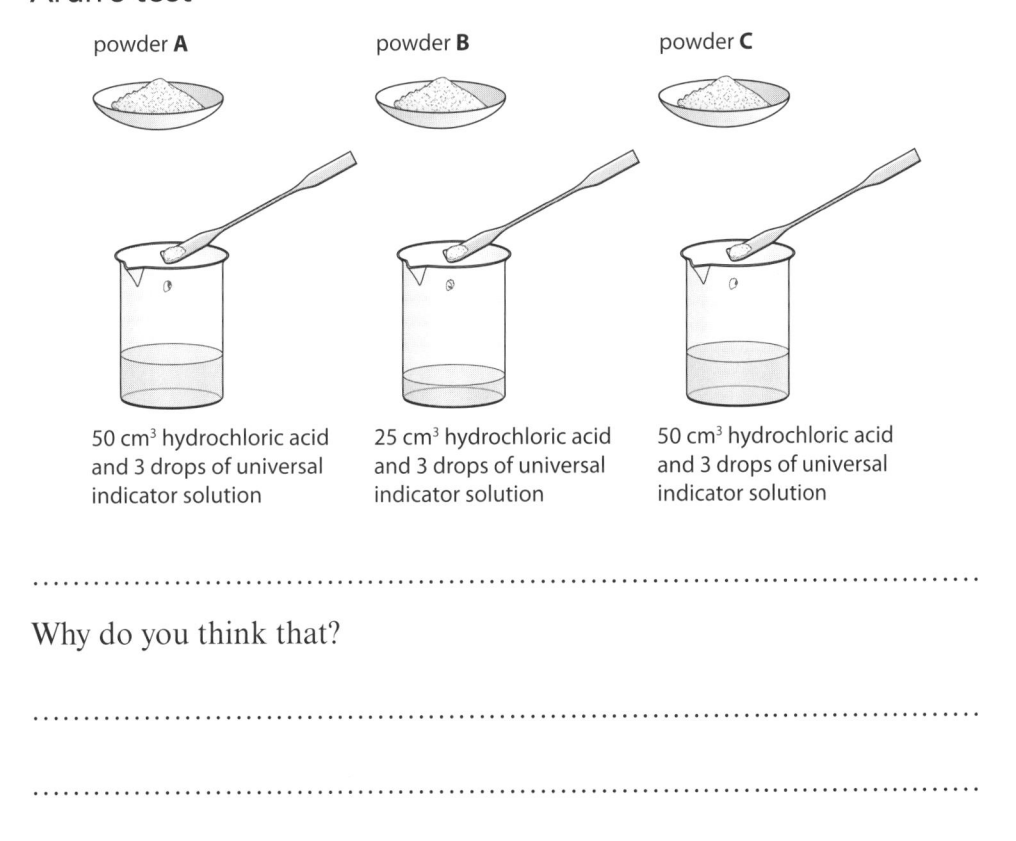

powder **A**   powder **B**   powder **C**

50 cm^3 hydrochloric acid and 3 drops of universal indicator solution

25 cm^3 hydrochloric acid and 3 drops of universal indicator solution

50 cm^3 hydrochloric acid and 3 drops of universal indicator solution

....

Why do you think that?

....

....

8 Changes to materials

Sofia's test

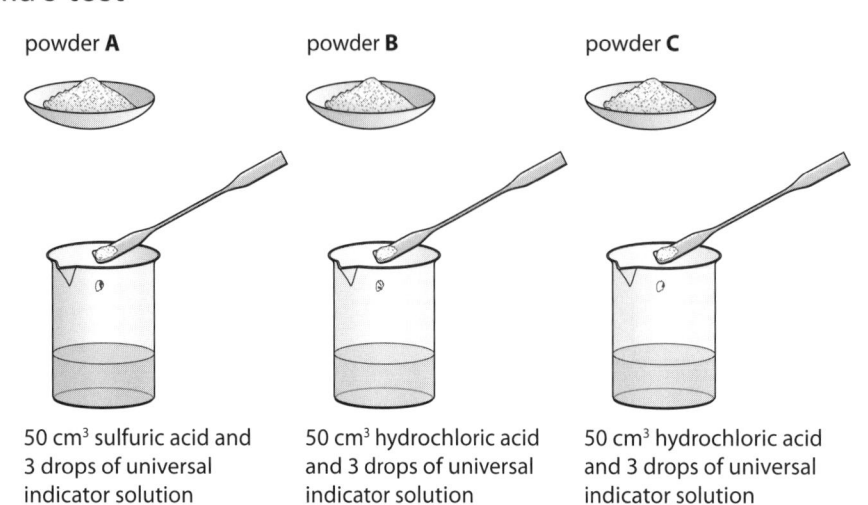

powder **A** powder **B** powder **C**

50 cm³ sulfuric acid and 3 drops of universal indicator solution

50 cm³ hydrochloric acid and 3 drops of universal indicator solution

50 cm³ hydrochloric acid and 3 drops of universal indicator solution

....

Why do you think that?

....

....

Zara's test

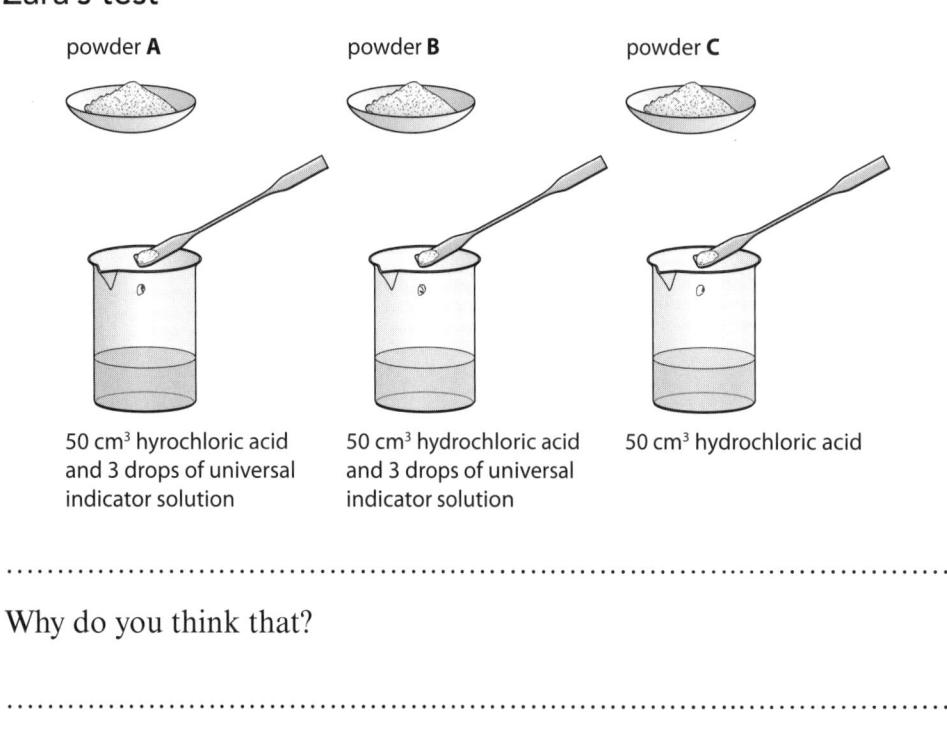

powder **A** powder **B** powder **C**

50 cm³ hyrochloric acid and 3 drops of universal indicator solution

50 cm³ hydrochloric acid and 3 drops of universal indicator solution

50 cm³ hydrochloric acid

....

Why do you think that?

....

....

8.3 Investigating acids and alkalis

Exercise 8.3B Planning investigations

Practice

This exercise will help you to think about how scientists plan and carry out investigations.

1. When scientists do experiments, they must think carefully about variables.

    Explain what a 'variable' is.

    ....

    ....

2. An environmental scientist tests the water from a number of lakes in the area where she works. The lakes have become acidic.

    The scientist needs to know which lake is the most acidic so that work can start on neutralising the acid.

Step 1

The scientist takes samples from each lake and tests them with universal indicator solution.

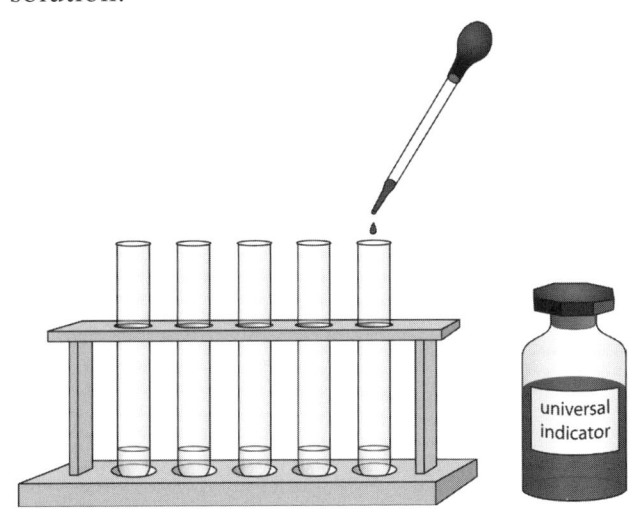

8 Changes to materials

Step 2

She adds sodium hydroxide solution to see how much is needed to neutralise the lake water.

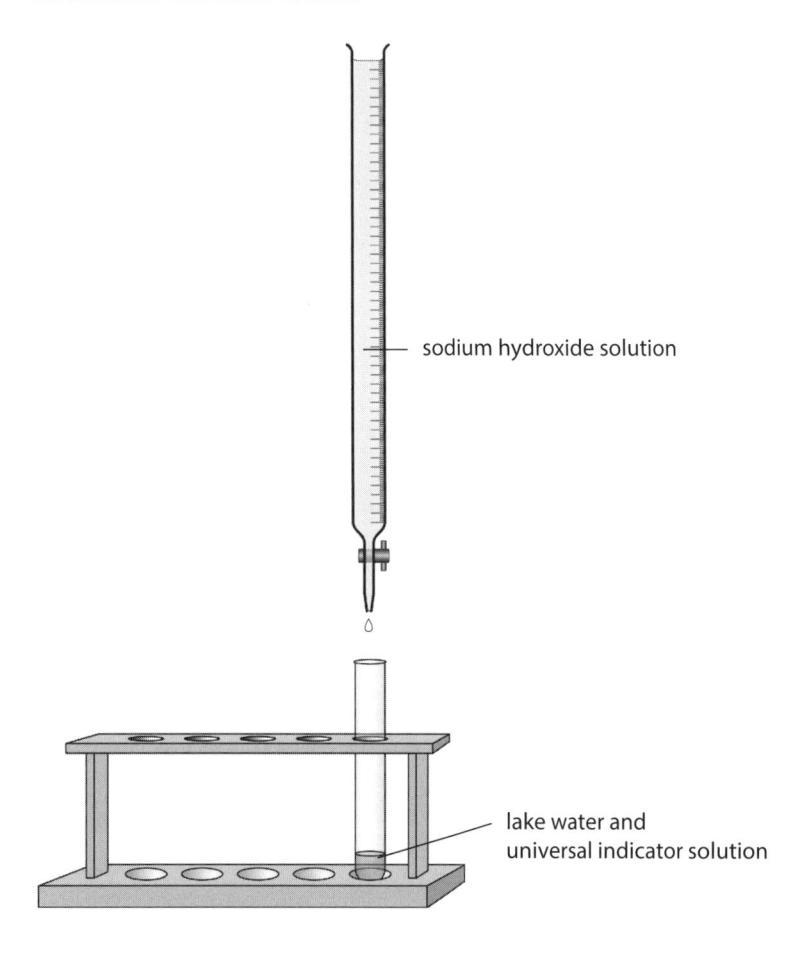

- sodium hydroxide solution
- lake water and universal indicator solution

a Explain what the scientist should do to make sure that she carries out a fair test in step 2.

....

....

b The scientist tests each sample three times. Explain why it is important to do this.

....

....

8.3 Investigating acids and alkalis

c The table shows the scientist's results.

Lake	Volume of sodium hydroxide needed to neutralise sample in cm³			
	First try	Second try	Third try	Mean
A	4	6	5	5
B	10	9	11	10
C	1	1	1	1

What do these results tell you about the acidity of the three lakes, A, B and C? Explain your answers.

....

....

....

....

8 Changes to materials

Exercise 8.3C Investigating antacids

Challenge

This exercise will help you to develop your scientific enquiry skills: recording data, plotting a graph and interpreting the results.

Arun and Zara investigate how effective medicines for indigestion are. They test five antacids to see how much acid they will neutralise.

They add 4 g of powdered antacid, 1 g at a time, to 25 cm³ of acid with pH of 2. After each addition of antacid they check the pH with a pH meter.

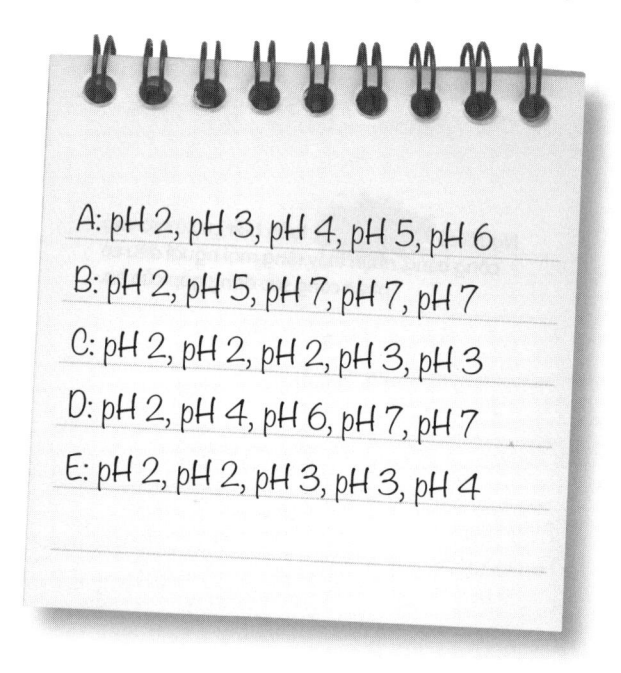

A: pH 2, pH 3, pH 4, pH 5, pH 6
B: pH 2, pH 5, pH 7, pH 7, pH 7
C: pH 2, pH 2, pH 2, pH 3, pH 3
D: pH 2, pH 4, pH 6, pH 7, pH 7
E: pH 2, pH 2, pH 3, pH 3, pH 4

1 Write the results in the table.

Antacid powder	pH				
	after 0 g	after 1 g			

2 On the grid below, label axes for mass of powdered antacid horizontally, and for pH vertically. Plot the results from the table to produce five separate line graphs, one for each of the five powders. Label each of the line graphs.

8 Changes to materials

3   Which variables did Arun and Zara keep the same to make this a fair test?

....

....

4   Which antacid(s) had the biggest effect on pH? ....

5   Which antacid(s) increased the pH most quickly? ....

6   Which antacid(s) had the least effect on pH? ....

7   What pH would you expect if you added 2.5 g of powder B to the acid? ....

8   Estimate what mass of powder A you would need to add to the acid to get a pH of 5.5 ....

9   The antacids that work very quickly produce a lot of gas quickly. Which would you choose as the ideal antacid? Give your reasons.

....

....

....

> 8.4 Detecting chemical reactions

Exercise 8.4A Key words for material changes

Focus

This exercise will help you to remember the meanings of words used in the chemical changes topic.

Draw lines to match each word with its meaning.

Word	Meaning
neutralisation	pH of less than 7
precipitate	able to dissolve or eat away other materials
pH scale	this is the name of the reaction where an acid is cancelled out by an alkali. A neutral solution has a pH of 7
corrosive	these are what you start with in a chemical reaction
reactants	pH of more than 7
products	this is what is formed when two liquids react and produce a solid
alkali	these are what is made in a chemical reaction
acid	this shows the strength of an acid or an alkali

8 Changes to materials

Exercise 8.4B Has a reaction taken place?

Practice

This exercise will help you to remember what to look for in deciding whether a reaction has taken place.

One of the ways you can tell that a reaction has taken place is if a gas is given off. You can tell because there will be bubbles or fizzing.

Example: vinegar and baking powder

Give three **other** things you should look for to tell if a reaction has happened. For each one, give an example.

First observation:

....

....

Example:

....

Second observation:

....

....

Example:

....

Third observation:

....

....

Example:

....

Exercise 8.4C Testing for gases

Challenge

This exercise will give you practice in describing the tests for gases.

You have four test tubes: one contains air, one oxygen, one hydrogen and one carbon dioxide. Your job is to find out which is which. Describe how you would do this.

9 Electricity

> 9.1 Flow of electricity

Exercise 9.1 The movement of electrons

In this exercise, you will describe how current flows.

Focus

1   Electrons are particles that can be found in wires.

    What happens to the electrons when current flows?

    Tick (✓) one box.

    The electrons vibrate more slowly. ☐

    The electrons do not move in the circuit. ☐

    The electrons flow around the circuit. ☐

    The electrons move randomly in the circuit. ☐

2   For each of these statements, write 'true' or 'false'.

    a   Electrons in wires are free to move. ....

    b   Electrons have a positive charge. ....

9.1 Flow of electricity

Practice

3 Complete the sentences. Use words from the list.

The words may be used once, more than once or not at all.

> neutral   positive   negative

a   A cell has a .... and a .... terminal.

b   In a circuit, electrons flow away from the .... terminal and towards the .... terminal.

Challenge

4 Look at the circuit.

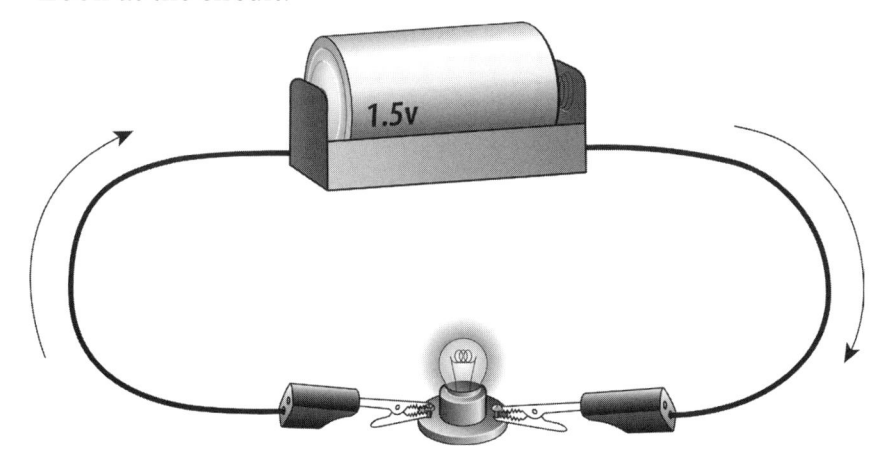

The arrows show the direction of electron flow.

Use these arrows to help you write + and − symbols on the cell in the correct places.

9 Electricity

> 9.2 Electrical circuits

Exercise 9.2 Circuits and symbols

In this exercise, you will use symbols to identify and draw circuits.

Focus

1   Write the names of the circuit symbols in the spaces beside the symbols.

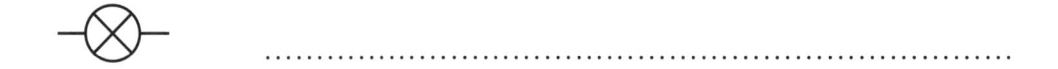

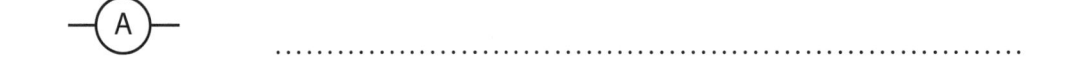

    ⊣⊢   ....

    ─⊗─   ....

    ─(A)─   ....

    ─o╱o─   ....

2   Which of these circuits will give light and sound a buzzer when the switch is closed?

    Tick (✓) one box.

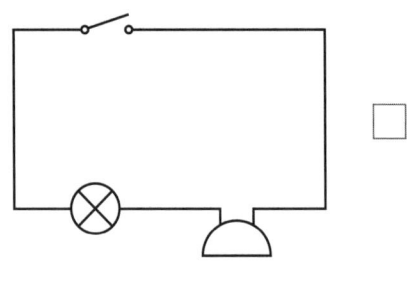

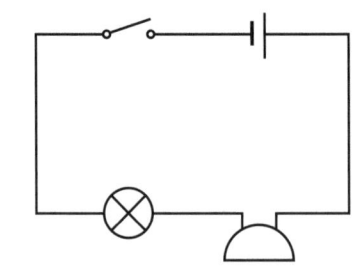

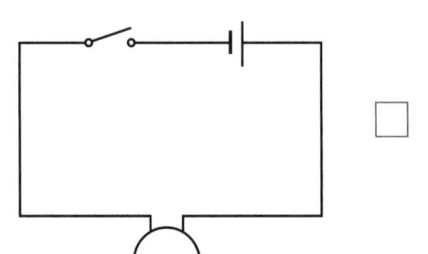

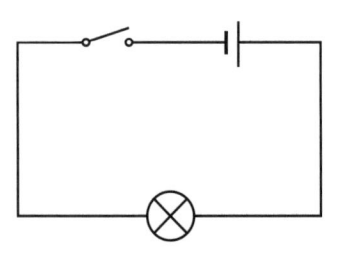

9.2 Electrical circuits

Practice

3 In the spaces provided, draw circuit diagrams for:

   a a series circuit with two cells, two lamps and a switch

   b a series circuit with one cell, one buzzer, one ammeter and a switch.

Challenge

4 Look at the two circuit diagrams, X and Y.

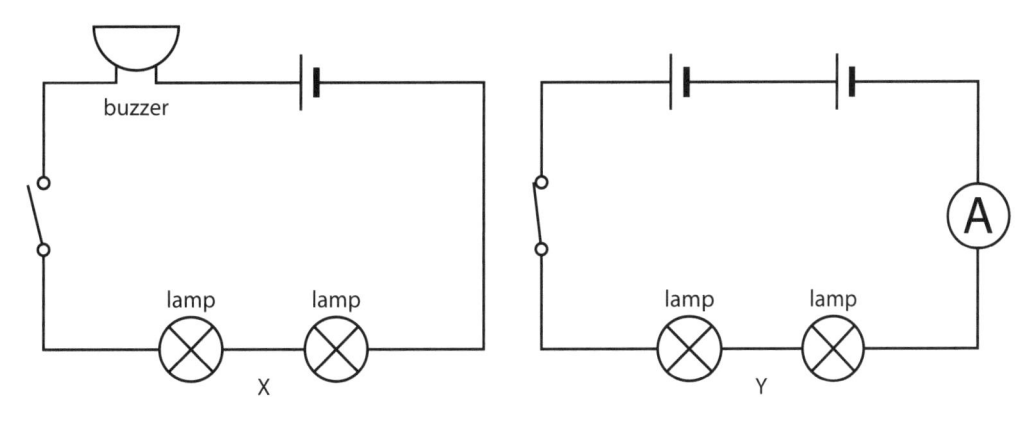

List **three** ways that circuit Y is different from circuit X.

   1 ....

   2 ....

   3 ....

9 Electricity

> 9.3 Measuring the flow of current

Exercise 9.3 Current in circuits

In this exercise, you will describe how current is measured.

Focus

1 Sofia measures the current in a circuit. She records the number 2 for the current. She does not use the unit.

   Circle the correct unit for current.

           C   A   V   N

2 Complete the sentence. Use the best word.

   When electrons flow faster in a circuit, the current is

   ....

Practice

3 Arun has a circuit with a cell and a lamp. He wants to use an ammeter to measure the current in the circuit.

   How should he connect the ammeter?

   Tick (✓) all boxes that are correct.

   anywhere in series with the cell and the lamp   ☐

   in series between the lamp and the positive of the cell   ☐

   in series between the lamp and the negative of the cell   ☐

   replace the lamp with the ammeter   ☐

9.3 Measuring the flow of current

Challenge

4 Sofia has a multimeter. A multimeter can be switched to make different electrical measurements.

Sofia switches her multimeter to measure current.

Look at the scale of the multimeter.

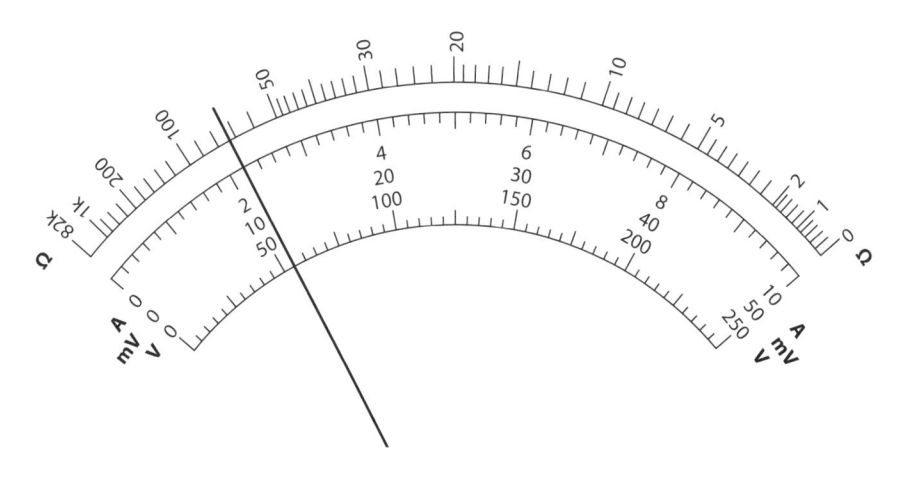

Which of these is the current in Sofia's circuit?

Circle the correct reading.

    60A   2.2A   12A   75A

9 Electricity

> 9.4 Conductors and insulators

Exercise 9.4 Allowing electrons to flow or inhibiting electrons from flowing

In this exercise, you will describe the differences between conductors and insulators.

Focus

1. Which of these materials is a good conductor of electricity?

   Underline one material.

           wood   plastic   metal   air

2. Which of these materials could **not** be used to make electric wires?

   Underline one material.

           steel   copper   cotton   aluminium

Practice

3. Zara is testing large objects to find out if they conduct electricity. She has a circuit with a cell, a lamp and two metal contacts.

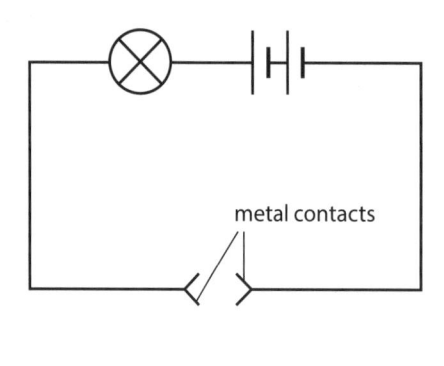

a When Zara touches the metal contacts to a large piece of iron, the lamp lights up.

Explain why.

....

....

b Zara knows that a car is made from steel. Zara touches the metal contacts to a car door. The lamp does **not** light.

Suggest why.

....

....

Challenge

4 Gold is one of the best electrical conductors.

Glass is one of the best electrical insulators.

Explain, in terms of electrons, the differences between gold and glass.

....

....

....

9 Electricity

> 9.5 Adding and removing components

Exercise 9.5 Changing the number of cells or lamps

In this exercise, you will explain the effect on current of changing components in a circuit.

Focus

1   Which component will **increase** the current when added correctly into a series circuit?

    Tick (✓) one box.

    cell   ☐
    lamp   ☐
    buzzer   ☐
    switch   ☐

2   Look at the circuit diagram.

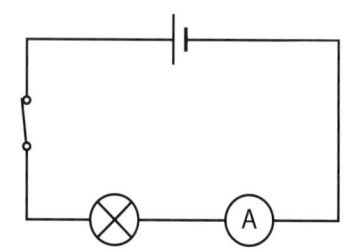

    The ammeter reads 0.6 A.

    Which of these components will **decrease** the current to 0.3 A when added in series?

    Tick (✓) one box.

    another identical cell   ☐
    another identical lamp   ☐
    another identical ammeter   ☐
    another identical switch   ☐

Practice

3 Marcus builds the circuit shown in the diagram.

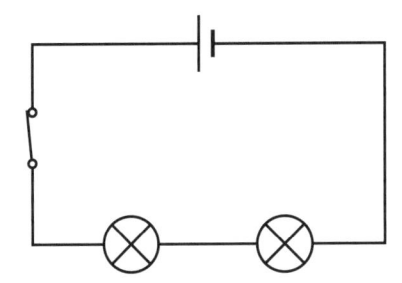

Marcus wants to increase the current in this circuit.
He has one more of each component.

Describe **two** ways he could increase the current in this circuit.

1 ....

2 ....

Challenge

4 a Explain why adding more cells into a series circuit will increase the current.

....

....

....

b Look at this circuit diagram.

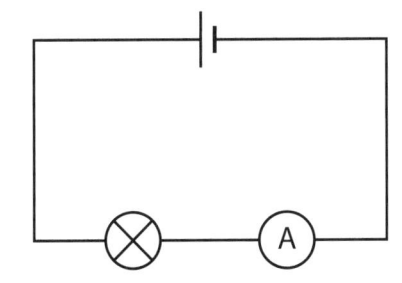

The reading on the ammeter is 2A.

9 Electricity

Suggest what the ammeter reading will be when there are:

i two identical lamps in the same circuit

....

....

ii three identical lamps in the same circuit.

....

....